promises a life of *abondanza,* as Kathy would say. The great news, as this delightful book shows us, is that a fully alive life is not just an Italian party; it's for the Irish, too, and for the Russian, German, Japanese, Iranian, and…"

—GLORIA GAITHER, lyricist, author, and speaker

"Kathy Troccoli lives life to the fullest. Whether singing to the masses in sold-out concerts or reaching out to children in remote African villages, Kathy seeks to bless others and, as she describes, 'to absorb the glory of every moment.' She not only absorbs it, she exudes it. Her stirring words will inspire readers to seize the life of passion, romance, and adventure that Christ freely offers."

—JAMES ROBISON, president and founder of LIFE Outreach International

"From her colorful Italian heritage to her present worldwide ministry, Kathy Troccoli is one of the finest, most enjoyable talents on stage today. With warmth, humor, charm, and incredible giftedness, my wonderful friend steals your heart. But there's so much more. She loves God, people, and life. Read all about it in *Live Like You Mean It.*"

—LUCI SWINDOLL, speaker and author of *I Married Adventure*

"Reading this book is like opening a box full of love letters. Kathy's passion for God spills off every page as she describes the richness of life He has given her. *Live Like You Mean It* is honest, unguarded, funny, and extremely inspirational as Kathy encourages all of us to experience how wonderful life can be if we trust God completely. I believe she means it."

—R. MARTIN COLEMAN, chief operating officer of FamilyNet Television

Praise for
Live Like You Mean It

"You'll search a long time before you find a sweeter heart, deeper fa
and better communicator than Kathy Troccoli. I've known her m
than a decade—she's a fresh voice for these tough times."

—MAX LUCADO, best-selling author of *It's Not About Me,*
When God Whispers Your Name, and other books

"*Live Like You Mean It* is the feel-good book of the season—filled v
vital girlfriend chatter and other melodious matters of a woman's he
Kathy's deep, rich, honest voice is matched by her radiant spiri
vigor for life! Enjoy!"

—PATSY CLAIRMONT, Women of Faith speaker
and author of *I Grew Up Little*

"It is a tragedy when we fail to live our one glorious life for some
or something less than Jesus. I know of no one I respect more for l
ing a rich, full, passionate, and Christ-centered life than Kathy Trocc
She invites us to the strength of faithfulness and the glorious sensu
ity of love. This is a book to savor as you marvel at the life God l
created for you to live."

—DAN B. ALLENDER PHD, president of Mars Hill Graduate School
and author of *The Wounded Heart* and *To Be Told*

"If there is anyone who swallows life in great gulps, it's Kathy Tro
coli. It's not just that she's Italian—though I admit that helps—b
also that she has chosen to follow a God who is not risk-free but wl

Live Like You Mean It

Live Like You Mean It

Seven Celebrations to Rejuvenate Your Soul

Kathy Troccoli

WATERBROOK
PRESS

LIVE LIKE YOU MEAN IT
PUBLISHED BY WATERBROOK PRESS
12265 Oracle Boulevard, Suite 200
Colorado Springs, Colorado 80921
A division of Random House Inc.

All Scripture quotations, unless otherwise indicated, are taken from the *Holy Bible, New International Version®*. NIV®. Copyright © 1973, 1978, 1984 by International Bible Society. Used by permission of Zondervan Publishing House. All rights reserved. Scripture quotations marked (MSG) are taken from *The Message*. Copyright © 1993, 1994, 1995, 1996, 2000, 2001, 2002. Used by permission of NavPress Publishing Group. Scripture quotations marked (NASB) are taken from the *New American Standard Bible®*. © Copyright The Lockman Foundation 1960, 1962, 1963, 1968, 1971, 1972, 1973, 1975, 1977, 1995. Used by permission. (www.Lockman.org). Scripture quotations marked (NKJV) are taken from the *New King James Version*. Copyright © 1982 by Thomas Nelson Inc. Used by permission. All rights reserved. Scripture quotations marked (TLB) are taken from *The Living Bible*, copyright © 1971. Used by permission of Tyndale House Publishers Inc., Wheaton, Illinois 60189. All rights reserved.

Details in some anecdotes and stories have been changed to protect the identities of the persons involved.

ISBN 1-4000-7161-5

Copyright © 2006 by Kathy Troccoli

All rights reserved. No part of this book may be reproduced or transmitted in any form or by any means, electronic or mechanical, including photocopying and recording, or by any information storage and retrieval system, without permission in writing from the publisher.

WATERBROOK and its deer design logo are registered trademarks of WaterBrook Press, a division of Random House Inc.

Library of Congress Cataloging-in-Publication Data
Troccoli, Kathy.
    Live like you mean it : seven celebrations to rejuvenate your soul / Kathy Troccoli.—1st ed.
        p. cm.
    Includes bibliographical references.
    ISBN 1-4000-7161-5
    1. Christian women—Religious life. I. Title.
    BV4527.T77 2006
    248.8'43—dc22

                                                                                2005022272

Printed in the United States of America
2006—First Edition

10 9 8 7 6 5 4 3 2 1

For Maria.
You inspire me.

Contents

Acknowledgments

To my editor, Traci Mullins—what an incredible gift you gave by pushing and motivating me to put so much of myself into this manuscript. You took the time to draw out every last bit of passion, romance, and adventure I had in me but hadn't fully expressed.

To Steve Cobb and my team at WaterBrook Press— Dudley, Brian, Alice, Laura, Ginia, Joel, and Jessica, I love it that you "get" me. Thanks for your partnership.

To my manager and agent, Matt Baugher—the adventure continues! I love that you also live life like you mean it. I can't wait for what's ahead.

To Deb Baugher—what a ceiling!

To Carol, Jen, Billye, and Thresa—your prayers and wisdom are priceless.

To Paris—thanks for noticing.

And to Allyson and Ellie—isn't God wonderful? I love you.

Somewhere Over the Rainbow

I find in myself a desire, which no experience in this world can satisfy. The most profitable explanation is that I was made for another world.

C. S. LEWIS
Mere Christianity

*P*aris called me the other day. At sixteen, my friend Ellie's daughter is a colorful teenager and quite an independent soul. I was a little surprised but complimented when she said she had a couple of questions to ask me and needed my advice. Most of the time I imagine she is thinking I'm either the biggest nerd or a pretty cool singer-friend of her mother's.

"Okay, Kathlini [her nickname for me], I am doing a report and I need a couple of adjectives to describe my parents. I thought you might be able to come up with some good ones for them. I have some, but they seem pretty boring. Can you help me?"

"Hmm… Well, Paris, let's see. I would say integrity for your dad. You know how he lives his life with the family and in business."

"Oh, yeah…good…that's a good one."

"And for your mom, I'd have to say that colorful would be at the top of my list. She is like a human kaleidoscope. Funny, intelligent, gregarious. You know how much she reminds us of Lucille Ball when she does crazy things." (When Ellie goofs off, Paris and her siblings usually roll their eyes, as teenagers will do, but I practically roll on the floor belly laughing.)

"Yeah. You're right. That's another good one."

I went on to suggest some more words for her parents, as well as for her brother and sister. It was endearing for me to hear her readily agree with the complimentary descriptions. We chatted for a few more minutes, and I was just about to say good-bye when Paris piped up.

"Do you know what adjective I would use for you, Kathlini?"

"Excuse me?"

"I have an adjective that describes you."

"Okay," I replied, a bit hesitantly.

"Rich. I think you are rich. I don't mean money rich. You are rich in your life—in your soul."

"Wow, Paris. Thank you. That really blesses me."

Outwardly I was trying to sound cool, but inside I was practically hyperventilating with awe: *She's been watching me that closely?* I didn't realize that this teenager I had known since her childhood even had an opinion about me. I closed my eyes and thanked God.

"Well…I'll see you soon," Paris said. "Love you. Bye."

I hung up the phone and let my young friend's words sink deep into my heart.

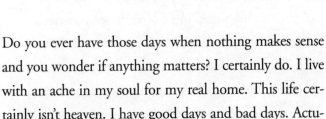

Do you ever have those days when nothing makes sense and you wonder if anything matters? I certainly do. I live with an ache in my soul for my real home. This life certainly isn't heaven. I have good days and bad days. Actually I have some really fabulous days and some really devastating ones. I even have days when I still question the point of my very existence.

But I do have a love for life—when I'm not wishing myself out of the discomfort of this world. I am eager to live my days with passion and a spirit of adventure. I am determined to live life richly and to let its bouquet romance my soul. I am committed to give life all I've got.

- I love to laugh till my belly hurts; I have cried as hard.
- I enjoy people, but they can hurt me.
- Friends love me, and I can hurt them.

- Bread comforts me. So does pizza…and Oreos. (But I hate how these delicacies can so easily end up around my thighs and my middle.)
- I love to sleep, but I hate the sound of the alarm clock.
- I am always amazed when the sun sets. I wish I got out of bed more often to see it rise.
- I work really hard, but I can play with just as much energy.

Life is fast and life is full. It brings enormous heartache but possesses a silencing beauty. I don't want to miss a thing.

I wasn't always this way. Living with a burning sense of purpose and enthusiastic zest for life is not my natural approach. Even though I've long been a fiery extrovert who loves to go for the gusto, my soul has always been laced with a certain melancholy. My upbringing in an Italian-American family did give me a lot of what you would expect from the stereotype of that background— like the loud way of expressing myself, which can sound like I'm angry, but I'm just being passionate about something. Oh, and the gigantic hugs. I remember when I first moved to Nashville in the early eighties, I invaded people's space all the time. I could tell by their body language and the looks on their faces. *Why is this woman I met two seconds ago hugging me and kissing me on the cheek?*

I quickly learned the art of air kissing, although I'm not very good at it. I still err on the side of invasion. My mother thought it rude and disrespectful if I didn't kiss and hug people every time I entered and left a room. It didn't matter if there was one person or fifty.

"Say good-bye to so-and-so, Kathleen."

At the time, I hated it. Especially men with scruffy beards and women drenched with nauseating perfume. Yuck. I didn't know them, and I didn't plan to see them again. But alas, it was the Italian way of life. I guess now I'm thankful for it, because it's given me an openness and a welcoming style to my personality that I wouldn't have had without my mother's prodding.

I grew up on Long Island, New York, amid my mother's side of the family—the Espositos, Gallellis, and Pellechias. My childhood world revolved around my cousins, especially Carmine and Dominick. I gravitated toward them because girl toys and games were so boring to me. Whatever we played, I got totally into it. I didn't just play my part, I became the part. Whether it was cowgirl, spy, or racecar driver, I wanted to be the best.

It didn't take me long to realize that I was quite different from my cousins. I thought about life and people more deeply and penetratingly than other kids did. I would cry a lot; I took things so hard.

Tempers flared often on our little Italian corner. Then there would be silence. Eventually, all would be well again—until the next episode. I would often wonder, with a heavy heart, *Why can't we get along?* I would internalize the ache.

This was true in relation to just about everything. The pain in the mundane of life would have its way with my soul and emotions. A wounded kitten or dog would throw me into depression. My mom's headache would make me run to the sink for a wet cloth and would leave me sick with worry. The sight of my grandma's scarred flesh on her arm from a childhood accident would break my heart.

Little did I know that the ache would remain into adulthood because I have a pulse and I am still on this earth. Little did I know that people would still fight and not say they are sorry. And many, many sights and sounds would still leave my heart in anguish.

Falling in love with Jesus didn't change my world, but it changed me and my perspective. I have gained more wisdom about this world and the things I cannot change, but I have also found some places where I can make my mark on eternity. I have a genuine love and compassion for people. Lots of pain and a little Italian heritage have increased my capacity to love. My sadness is often soothed by His grace and faithfulness—and by remembering to have a thankful heart. I can trust Him when I'm completely mystified. I can find comfort when I yearn for a glimpse of the other side. I know that eternity will hold my final answers. I'll probably have no need then to ask the questions. And most of all, I'll stop crying.

I don't think Paris would have called me rich if I didn't know Jesus. More than half my lifetime ago I asked Jesus to come into my heart. I initially loved Him just because I understood what He did for me, and at that point I couldn't possibly ignore it. But I believe I love Him now far more than I did in my honeymoon time. He holds out hope and I strive to hang on to it. He makes me believe that I'm going to make it—and I see that I do. He gives me my sanity—on my own, I tend to get awfully confused. He breathes life into me when I feel empty. He gives me perspective. I am so in need of His wisdom. He fills me with love—I run out so quickly.

Jesus said, "I came so they can have real and eternal life, more and better life than they ever dreamed of" (John 10:10, MSG). His words were deliberate. His promises are certain. Will I read them as though they were only lofty poetry or excerpts from a fairy tale? Or will I take them deep into my heart and live in anticipation of how they will come true in my life? *More and better life than I ever dreamed of.*

I will never forget the first time I saw *The Wizard of Oz* and how moved I was, even at age seven, by Judy Garland's yearning for a life beyond what she knew on the farm in Kansas:

When all the clouds darken up the skyway
There's a rainbow highway to be found
Leading from your windowpane
To a place beyond the sun

Just a step behind the rain
Somewhere over the rainbow
Skies are blue
And the dreams that you dare to dream
Really do come true[1]

As a child on Long Island, I loved the summer nights and the breeze we enjoyed since we lived so close to the ocean. I would often look up at the brilliant stars in the sky and wonder…

- *What is beyond the stars?*
- *What is beyond the moon?*
- *What is beyond what I can see?*

Never would I have imagined the life that awaited me. Nor could I have known, except in hindsight, that God only reveals what we need to see at the moment. He gives the measure of grace we need for the measure of our pain. And that pain—if we let it—molds in us the heart that God longs for us to have.

No eye has seen,
 no ear has heard,
no mind has conceived

what God has prepared for those who love
him. (1 Corinthians 2:9)

The God who made heaven and earth is an amazing planner. We forget that. And furthermore, we want to be in on the plan from the get-go. Or, we set the agenda and tell the Lord to adjust heaven and earth to fit the plans we have made. How many of us lead a life on the sidelines of the greatest life God yearns to give us because we have taken our own path? We settle for crumbs and miss out on the feast.

There is no end to what God Almighty can do. The only ones who put stop signs on the roads to His glory are you and I. It is because we are busy believing out of our brokenness. Questioning out of our pain. Grumbling out of our selfishness. Loving out of our own desperate need to be loved.

- Are there chains on the hands that created the heavens?
- Are there blinders on the eyes that saw you in the womb?
- Are there straps on the arms of the One who rolled the stone away?

What a very short time we have here. Even if we live to be a hundred years old, it goes by in the blink of an eye.

- How will we live?
- What will we believe?
- What will we be remembered for?

We've all heard the popular phrase, "Life is hard and then you die." No! I say, "Life is hard, but you can live!"

In his letter to some of the early Christians, the apostle Paul said something so beautiful: "I pray that you, being rooted and established in love, may have power, together with all the saints, to grasp how wide and long and high and deep is the love of Christ, and to know this love that surpasses knowledge—that you may be filled to the measure of all the fullness of God" (Ephesians 3:17-19).

The *fullness of God*. Can you imagine? Oh, how I yearn for that in my heart and in my life! It is there for my taking.

I remember how much I listened to the late Keith Green in the seventies and early eighties. He was a brilliant songwriter. In my early years with the Lord, Keith's music penetrated my soul. One of his lyrics says:

Jesus rose from the grave

And you, you can't even get out of bed![2]

I wanted so badly back then to live a passionate life with Him and for Him. And I still do, even though I have experienced periods of slumber. A few years ago I started practicing seven powerful intentions that God revealed to me as I sought to engage in a life of passion, romance, and adventure—the life I believe He wants for all of us. I affectionately call them Seven Celebrations to Rejuvenate Your Soul. They actually take a good deal of discipline to incorporate into one's life, but they ultimately cause the soul to celebrate—to experience life to its fullest potential, to live "over the rainbow" in the here and now. Here they are:

1. Live *La Dolce Vita*
2. Fill Up on the Finest
3. Keep Your Life Web Free
4. Talk to God
5. Stay Ripe for the Picking
6. Wait in Expectation
7. Be a Desperate Woman

We *can* live somewhere over the rainbow in this life, and definitely in the next. We have so many riches—

treasure upon treasure waiting to be discovered. We can catch glimpses of God as our hearts become clear enough to see Him. I want to doubt Him less and love Him more, don't you?

We can believe beyond what we understand. We can experience the powerful presence of our Creator and bask in His love beyond anything we can imagine. I want to stay within the lines of His highway and enjoy the freedoms in the narrow road. A challenging journey for my flesh. A big adventure for my soul.

I invite you to read the pages ahead as if we are taking a long drive together. Along the way, we'll seize the life of passion, romance, and adventure. Let's discover what it means to live like you mean it. We'll put in some great CDs but probably keep turning the volume down because there is so much to talk about. Come on! Let's go…

Live La Dolce Vita

It is not how much we have, but how much
we enjoy, that makes happiness.

CHARLES HADDON SPURGEON

I love food! We had macaroni every Sunday and my mother's gravy (sauce) was the best. Isn't every Italian mother's sauce the best? Food was celebration. Food was joy. Food was conversation. Food was laughter. To sit around the table for six hours with a few television and bathroom breaks was standard operating procedure for my Big Fat Italian Family.

I ate out recently at an Italian restaurant that was the real deal. The waiter had a thick accent, Frank Sinatra was playing, and the maître d' came by to offer a warm welcome.

"Señora, howa you do tonighda?"

Ahh, the familiar sound brought tears to my eyes. I wanted to kiss and hug him, even though he had a scruffy beard.

What Italians call *la dolce vita*—the sweet life—has always held great appeal for me. My colorful, boisterous, and emotionally erratic family birthed in me a ferocious appetite for *abondanza*—abundance, plenty, more of everything. More food. More music. More dancing. More jokes. More arguments. More tears. More heartache. More laughter. Just more.

As I continued to grow up, I became the dreamer of the family who believed that la dolce vita was actually attainable and sustainable. That illusion really was "over the rainbow" because life, of course, contains both the bitter and the sweet. When sorrow not only rained but poured, I became more and more disillusioned, even depressed.

It wasn't until young adulthood that I learned about God's version of la dolce vita. His bold statements about the abundant life and what I could feel and experience in my deepest soul, regardless of circumstances, buoyed me. Whether in joy or pain, I could possess supernatural virtues and enjoy sweet communion with my Creator from now into eternity. The sweet life was no longer out of reach. As a child of God, I only needed to lift my sights and remember that every promise He has made is a promise kept. The sweet life is no longer a party, or a place, or people that are fond of me on a certain day. La dolce vita is within me, because the Holy Spirit has decided to miraculously dwell there.

I visited friends and family on Long Island recently. My good friend Salvatore Massa picked me up to have a Sunday dinner with the Aniellos. Linny had promised me pasta and sausage and meatballs, so my mouth was watering in anticipation of a good Italian home-cooked meal. Since moving south (please excuse me, my southern friends), I crave what I took for granted in New York. Ahh, a bagel store and pizzeria on every corner. Italian delis and bakeries available to your hearts content. But now I often hear, "There is a good Eye-talian restaurant in…"

Need I say more?

I never go over to someone's home for a meal without bringing something. Momma Troccoli instilled that in me when I was a little girl.

"It's rude to show up with nothing in your hands, Kathleen."

So I asked Sal to stop at a bakery before we dined at the Aniellos' house. When we walked into Villa Bella's, I was immediately enveloped by the sights and smells. Long loaves and short loaves and round loaves of bread.

The kind that is perfectly crusted on the outside and soft and warm on the inside. The shelves of the glass counters were lined with pastries, coffee was perking, and espresso was brewing—all reminders of the spread on the table through most of my childhood. I bent down as my eyes feasted on the colors and textures of the cannolis and pignoli cookies and napoleons. My visual ecstasy was interrupted when bursting from the kitchen came a tiny Italian woman smiling from ear to ear and wearing an apron spotted with flour.

"Sally boy! How you do? You wanna tasta anytinga? *Mangia!* Here-a! Eeeda!"

As I more than tasted, and Sal engaged this generous soul in animated conversation, I was taken by her hard-working hands and her soft heart. Inviting. Warm. Stuff that makes the world go 'round. I miss that kind of abandon in greeting others. I wanted to hug her and take her home.

In the midst of cell phones and e-mails and pagers, we're losing the art of conversation. We've stopped reaching out to the person we don't know. And we miss so much. Those are the ways God shows Himself to us and to others. Those are the very ways God increases our hearts' capacity to a size that makes room for Him. When we generously share a word, a thought, or a story, our hearts enlarge. Our own experiences can jade us, leaving us judgmental and close minded. When we participate in sweet moments with others, however, we beautify the landscape of our own territories. We see farther and feel deeper.

At the core of the sweet life is the enjoyment of people. Participating in their lives in ways that bless and encourage and lift up. This exchange most of the time will present itself in unexpected places. I am frequently in airports, and at any gate in any airport right now you will see more people engaging with technology than with another human soul. Then we wonder why some of our kids just grunt at us and our guests. Many of us grownups have become apathetic and self-absorbed, never even entertaining the thought of just asking people how they are.

It was quite common years ago to sit on a porch at the close of a day. Young mothers asked advice from the lady next door. Kids played with actual toys and used their imaginations. "Game boys" were nothing more than children playing—not robotic kids losing a sense of life and time and relationship because a tiny machine in their hands hypnotically entrances them. Don't get me wrong. It is all exciting and cool and fun. But somehow we are losing balance. We're falling off the edge of the mountaintops from which God has designed for us to have clear vision. That is where we will keep a passionate heart about His concerns for the world and for one another. We lose that, and we will slowly lose our souls.

I was at a Subway sandwich shop in Nashville recently and ran into my friends Dick and Melody Tunney. It was a beautiful sunny day, and they were having lunch with their two twentysomething daughters. I watched them through the window as they sat at a table outside and talked. It was clear that they were thoroughly enjoying one another.

As I left, I took the time to tell them how encouraging it was for me to see them chatting away. I told them how unique I thought that was in this day and age. It was glorious to witness the sweet life through this family. Simply and purely. It was a drastic difference from the day before at Borders bookstore. A man and a woman sipping coffee at a table with their daughter. The entire time they sat there, the daughter talked nonstop on her cell phone. The parents seemed numb and used to it. It saddened my heart.

Life flies by, time ticks away, and we miss out on all the richness of love we could be sharing with one another. Most of the time it takes awareness to stop the slippage. Sometimes it takes work. But you will find yourself a wealthy person when you arrive in heaven if you're willing to grasp la dolce vita now.

For where your treasure is, there your heart
will be also. (Matthew 6:21)

After the luscious dinner at the Aniellos, Linny suggested a walk down the block. "There's a street festival going on, and besides, you have to meet Joe."

It turned out that it was Joe from Joe's Italian Market. He had just moved out to Long Island from Brooklyn. His store was filled with provolone and mozzarella and assorted salamis and steaks. Olives in bowls to be ordered by the pound and olive oil in cans and jars were on the shelves. Baci, Torrone, and Toblerone were there in abundance—all Italian candy that would delight anyone's palate.

With a handsome face and thick accent, Joe sang and danced as music blasted on the street. People joined him and so did I. Beyond his little party I noticed that his sons were cooking sausage and peppers on a huge grill. Joe was pleased to give the food away if people entered into his celebration. I loved watching Joe just celebrating life. No specific reason. Just life and love and his new friends.

It's amazing how often God gives food away as we enter into His celebration. The bread of heaven comes down. Nourishes our souls. Keeps our hearts healthy.

La dolce vita is the life that God grants to us when we focus on His Son. A life centered on what pleases Him, keeping an eye out for His take on things. Living in ways that He said would make us rich and bring us joy: humble, selfless, forgiving. Dying to live—truly live. Coming up from our sorrows to breathe in the love that will never let us go.

When we get tired and don't want to move on, Jesus is the One that we can hold on to because He knows no weariness. Besides that, He hasn't told us the end of our story yet. Our personal story can have a glorious ending. He promises us that and encourages us to keep on living just because He is alive and will give us everything that He is. It is a matter of the soul. Amidst the pain. Amidst the uncertainties. There is a good life. There is a great life. A peace beyond understanding. A knowing that all will be well. It's only found in Jesus.

Every year my parents and my sister, Jennifer, and I would drive into Brooklyn to spend New Year's with my dad's side of the family—the Troccolis, Sorannos, Terranovas, and DeMarias. It was the highlight of my year. Back then, two days felt like an eternity. I couldn't wait to be with my cousins.

When midnight approached, we would crowd around the television in eager anticipation of watching the ball drop over our beloved city.

"10, 9, 8, 7…Happy New Year!"

The noise was deafening but, oh, so delightful. Confetti filled the air like a sudden snowstorm. Hugs and kisses were exchanged for about ten minutes. Talk about love in the room. It was glorious. Spoons banged on pots and pans. Noisemakers (my personal favorite) added to the commotion. We would then parade into the street. My aunt Molly's neighbors must have thought, *It's those crazy Italians again!*

By the time we "little" cousins went to bed, it was around two in the morning. I could still hear the voices of my dad's brothers and cousins playing cards. I could see their white muscle T-shirts and their thick gold chains around their necks and, yes, the gold pinky rings. I could smell their potent cigars. The smoke would make its way up the stairs to where I was sleeping. It all kept me up for a while, but it also strangely comforted me. No, it wasn't quite a lullaby, but that aroma was like music to my ears. To this day, I love the smell of cigars.

Now that I live in Nashville, I still visit my aunt Molly, as well as my aunt Sherubina and clan back on Long Island. I love sharing a meal at Aunt Sherubina and Uncle Pasquale's house with all my cousins. We grew up together like siblings. I lived next door, and another aunt lived on the other side.

It is always quite an experience to go back home. I am transported quickly into the thick of accents, large hand movements to explain everything, and an overall decibel of talking that can lead one to deafness if not careful. I love my family, and there is still a big part of them inside of me.

I can sit there for hours listening to new tales of happenings with all the Italians. They are very much one another's social life, so they are filled with stories. I am always quite entertained to say the least, and I laugh till my belly hurts. One time when I visited my cousin Pattiann, I noticed that she had a tight Ace bandage wrapped around her wrist. I asked what had happened. She said she and my aunt Sherrie had rolled five pounds of meatballs one night, a common occurrence since thirteen people live in the house. They covered them and put them in the refrigerator overnight. When it came time to put them in the sauce the next day, she reached into the refrigerator with her right arm and fractured her wrist lifting them out!

My sister, Jennifer, lives very close to Aunt Sherubina, so she visits often. My niece Maria was home for a break from Bible school, so they went over for a meal. Maria is adorable around them. She talks freely about her life and love for Jesus and always asks to say the blessing over the food. If my family prays before they eat, they will recite the traditional Catholic blessing I said growing up:

Bless us, dear Lord,
and these Thy gifts
which we are about to receive
from Thy bounty,
through Christ our Lord.
Amen.

Usually before the "amen" is said, the food is being inhaled.

Maria offered to say the blessing last Thanksgiving. She went on and on. It was quite lovely, but I knew everyone was getting antsy. Her prayer was interrupted by my cousin Carmine. "Hurry up! I'm gettin' anorexic here!"

Laughter erupted.

Anyway, Maria had taken a mission trip to Mexico with students at her school. Now, this Thanksgiving, everyone had eaten and scattered to different places for a little while. She came in the house from being outside with her cousins, and there was a redness all over the palms of her hands. She showed it to my sister who in turn showed it to Uncle Pasquale. Do you remember in the movie *My Big Fat Greek Wedding* when the father used Windex as a cure-all for everything? Well, Uncle Pat's cure-all is rubbing (isopropyl) alcohol. Whenever there was an incident when I was a kid, he had the bottle in hand. Sometimes we would scram like the Road Runner before he got his hands on us. When he poured it on deep cuts it felt like you were losing a limb, but I must admit it cured many an ailment.

Of course, when Maria showed my uncle the rash on her hands, he got up to get his medicine. As he was looking for it, everyone heard him muttering, "I knew it! Ya had ta go outta the country? Ya neva know what you'll pick up! I can't believe ya let huh go ova dare! Look at dis rash! Let's hope id dusn't spread!"

Maria surrendered her hands to my well-intentioned uncle. As he rubbed the alcohol on her palms, everyone witnessed Uncle Pat's miracle healing. It started to wipe off! Maria then realized she had been leaning back on a freshly painted rust stoop outside the front door.

My family is a sitcom. Once again, there was enormous laughter.

There is so much color, texture, and emotion packed into the moments of life! Yet we miss the vita in the moments because we surrender our minds and hearts to the invasion and occupation of our worst enemies: worry, anxiety, resentment, shame. When these visitors take up residence, there is room for nothing else. We laugh less. Give less. Experience the fullness of la dolce vita less.

One woman I know refuses to miss out on the moments. My friend Luci Swindoll is the coolest seventy-three-year-old non-Italian I have ever met. She, in her own words, wants to "live the life out of every day." I was somewhat intimidated the first time I met Luci. She has a deep voice and enough southern charm to fill a room. She is so comfortable in her skin. Nothing seems to rattle her. She sees the adventure in every moment and wants to take the ride. Because she knows to whom she belongs, a refreshing confidence radiates from her. Luci lives life well—passionately, romantically, and adventurously. I wasn't surprised when she first told me she was going to write a book called *I Married Adventure*.

- Luci loves to travel the world and has been on all seven continents.
- She is well read.

- She is eloquent.
- She lights up like a child at the tiniest pleasure or gift.
- She treasures her photographs and finds joy in the capturing of a moment.
- She has a robust laugh.
- She laughs at herself.
- She tells a story, and you hang on every word.
- She speaks her mind.
- She is the embodiment of la dolce vita.

I think she would have loved to have been at the table recently when I took my sister and two of my cousins to lunch at Applebee's. After we had eaten our meal, I asked if anyone wanted dessert. They went back and forth and debated between several mouth-watering offers. I stopped their deliberation by ordering the entire dessert menu! They objected like I was crazy, but I could tell that even the thought of such an adventurous indulgence delighted their souls. They giggled and became little girls. I smiled as people gawked at us and watched us relish the moment.

Living la dolce vita doesn't require lots of money. Of course, people who have a lot of it can experience things that others just don't have the funds to do. If you have the funds, then go for it—and be sure to take others with you. But it's not about money. It's about the riches in the simple things. Your life can be lavish with simple riches:

- Light some candles during *any* meal.
- Pour your afternoon soft drink into the loveliest, most elegant glass you own.
- Place a bright flower in a vase on your kitchen table.
- Buy your favorite magazine and sit at Starbucks for a half hour.
- Take time for gazing—at the sunrise as well as the expression on children's faces.
- Dance with the kids in the living room.
- Take in colors and textures—a stroll down the street, an art gallery (they are usually free), the changes in the seasons.
- Jump into the pool with the kids.
- Send a sweet card in the mail.
- Take a walk and talk on a still night.
- Blast your favorite CD throughout the house.
- Make a quick call just to say "I love you."
- Take in the sights and smells and sounds that go largely unnoticed on any given day.

- Look up! Take time to notice the sky, whether it's cloudy or sunny.
- Notice the smells around you: coffee, flowers, Italian food cooking.
- Listen to the laughter of children, the birds, and the wind.

I love this verse in *The Message* Bible:

Who out there has a lust for life?
> Can't wait each day to come upon beauty?
>> (Psalm 34:12)

Take in every opportunity to make memories, because the moments don't come around again. God gives new opportunities every day, but yesterday never comes back. Don't miss a thing. Grab the moments. Celebrate them. When you do, you will not only feel alive, but you will also blow life into the sails of those around you.

Several years ago I was asked to perform on a cruise sponsored by Women of Faith. I invited my friend Ellie Lofaro (Paris's mom) as my guest. After dinner one night, Barbara Johnson asked us to meet her at her room at about eleven o'clock. She said she had a gift to give us. I was honored and had come to appreciate Barbara so much. She is a best-selling Christian author, but that to me is the least of her accolades. She has been through pain few have known and continues to adore Jesus and trust Him. At the same time, her humor puts a smile on thousands of faces. She lives to encourage. She intentionally embraces la dolce vita—the life of passion, romance, and adventure—at every opportunity.

Ellie and I made our way through the halls of the ship and found her room. We knocked on the door, and as long as I live, I will never forget the moments that ensued. The sliding doors that led to the balcony were open, so when she opened the door, a warm gust of wind blew upon us. Barbara's hair is always perfectly coifed, but that evening it had obviously been combed out. As the wind ran through it, she seemed much more vulnerable to me. It was like a Hollywood film from the fifties. She had on a brightly colored, floral satin robe, and on her feet were those puffy, furry kind of slippers. She warmly invited us in.

"The gift I have for you is outside. Follow me." She led us onto the balcony and told us to look up at the sky. She then told us to look through her husband's high-powered telescope, which was pointed toward the moon. It was bright, big, and perfectly round.

"Here's your present," she uttered with a giggle.

Suddenly the sky belonged to us. Every star seemed to twinkle with a little more beauty than I had ever seen. The water was glistening, and the sound of the waves was background music to what Barbara began reciting. It was from the poignant hymn, "The Love of God."

> Could we with ink the ocean fill
> And were the skies of parchment made
> Were every stalk on earth a quill
> And every man a scribe by trade
> To write the love of God above
> Would drain the ocean dry
> Nor could the scroll contain the whole
> Though stretched from sky to sky

Ellie and I didn't say a word. We all just stayed there awhile, leaning on the railing with our faces catching the wind. It touched our cheeks as the voice of God touched our hearts.

Whenever I hear the phrase "a life well lived," whether at a eulogy or a roast or an anniversary, it sparks something in me. It ignites a fire within me. It is a defining statement that I would love to hear said after my name. Whether now or when God chooses to take me home, how great it would be: *Kathy Troccoli. Hers was a life well lived.*

You know how when you look up something in the dictionary and it's described in full detail? Oh, to get to the end of my life here and look up Kathy Troccoli in Webster's and find descriptions like these:

- rich in relationships
- loves unconditionally
- known for generosity
- displays a gracious countenance
- possesses a welcoming heart
- quickly repents
- stores up an abundance of warm memories
- consistent in conviction
- extends mercy and compassion
- overtly kind in word and deed

- laughs a lot
- bold and courageous (willing to take risks)

Because of my singing and speaking, you must know that I have a heart for people. I often see myself bent on blowing winds of hope into the sails of the hurting and the brokenhearted and those without hope. Much of my compassion comes from the fact that I have had enormous pain in my own life. The loss of my parents, my ten-year struggle with bulimia, my all-out battle with depression, and my claiming bankruptcy at the age of thirty—all of that has given me a right to speak about life's devastations and also about the comfort that Jesus delivers. I yearn to give people hope and the unction to breathe another breath at the start of a new day. I simply give them what has been given to me.

I am convinced that the Lord keeps writing all of our stories, and He often uses pain as the ink in His pen. Before we know it, the chapters are filled with revelations and testimonies of His goodness and of how our hearts became a little bit bigger and our voices became a little bit stronger.

I know that I possess an ability to extend mercy that goes beyond my natural ability to feel. It is one of those supernatural happenings in my heart that can only come from a God who delivers supernatural virtues into our natural existence. The sorrow has stretched my heart to the point that I thought it would burst, only to find that He eventually increased my compassion and my ability to love in that very stretching.

I say all this to tell you more about Ellie. We have been the best of friends for fifteen years, and I still marvel at the way she attacks life. Of course, we have seen each other's potholes and have ridden on some bumpy roads because of them, but who hasn't when you are close to someone? The rocking and shaking has always challenged us to look at our pride. We both can be stubborn—throw in a little Italian seasoning and it makes for quite a colorful and amazing journey.

Ellie has a different bent toward people than I have. Whether it's the FedEx guy or the grocery clerk or the person sitting next to her on an airplane, she truly yearns for them to know the reality of Christ. Somehow the conversation will always lead there. Of course, I think about that when I meet people and interact with them, but it is not the overriding concern of my heart. Sure, I would love for everyone to have a personal relationship with Jesus, but for Ellie it is top priority. She has one of the biggest evangelist hearts I know.

I must confess that sometimes it can be frustrating. Ellie, her husband, Frank, and I will be out having dinner, and within five minutes, Ellie is engrossed in conversation with the waiter. It will most often result in the person's talking about where he or she is or isn't, spiritually. Frank and I will shake our heads knowing there is nothing we can do to stop her. Ellie is a Barbara Walters with an evangelical mission. She longs for people to know the riches that can be found in Jesus. We have seen her interview the hardest of hearts. Most people like to talk about themselves if they are pursued. Soon a person opens up a little and a life is touched—sometimes changed.

Frank and I will usually converse and let Ellie do her thing because we know she is sincere. That particular soul really does matter to her. Ellie looks at it as giving someone the most valuable and eternal gift that can ever be offered. I've seen her overturn some hard, rough soil— making a heart ready for God to throw whatever seed He chooses to sprinkle upon it. It usually only takes a small amount of conversation. Ellie is bold. She's courageous. Spending time with her through the years has felt like taking repeated trips to Disney World. You never know what adventure the day will hold.

When Ellie first moved from Long Island to Reston, Virginia, several years ago, she was a fish out of water. Virginia isn't actually the Deep South, but to an Italian New Yorker it is. After living in Reston only a few months, Ellie called me with an idea she had. She was going to knock on every door on her block and invite women to a Bible study. Needless to say, I thought it was pretty daring considering the majority of us barely wave at our neighbors. She told each woman that she had found the Bible to be life-giving and that it would be helpful to their lives.

The next week she was sitting with two women in her living room. That gathering has now grown to include more than one hundred women and meets every week in a local church.

It didn't surprise me a bit when Ellie eventually wrote a book called *Bonding with the Blonde Women*. Bold? Yes. Risky? Yes. Exciting? Yes! It is utterly amazing what God will do if we just step forward and reach out.

A couple of years ago, I went on a mission trip to South Africa. I was blessed to be part of a team from LIFE Outreach International that was feeding families and witnessing the drilling of water wells that could potentially be used for one thousand villagers for a lifetime. I could write a book on my experiences there and the profound ways God spoke to me. I was privileged to spend time with Peter and Ann Pretorius, a couple who led a program to feed and clothe hundreds of thousands of destitute people in Africa and other parts of the world.

One day as Ann and I were taking a lunch break out in the bush, we had a powerful conversation. It has stayed with me and gives me a heart to be bold and courageous.

"Kathy, have you ever been to Disney World?" Ann asked in her beautiful, regal South African accent.

"Oh, yes. Several times."

"You know, Kathy, I visited there when Peter and I were in America. It was absolutely fascinating to me. I thought, *If this could happen with one man and one mouse, what could happen with one woman and God?*"

Instead of reaching for God's possibilities, most of us tend to do the day-in, day-out routine and sometimes end up despising it. We don't give ourselves an outlet for new life to invade our souls. We don't let the flickers of good dreams and desires catch fire to set our world ablaze with zest and joy. The fear of rejection keeps us from moving forward in so many areas of our lives. The concern of what others may think about us and the constant voice of doom weighs us down before we even make a move to go to higher places.

Living like you mean it involves risk and requires courage—dreaming big. Constantly growing, seeing, experiencing. Going out of your comfort zone to start a conversation. Taking steps to go to higher places where you can truly do what you love to do. I love this anonymous quote:

> What would you do in life if you knew you could not fail?

That is not to say that all of us will grab the brass ring. But we will grab hold of the best of la dolce vita in the process. The hope, the courage, the strength. The journey will be rich and it will be full. True substance and character will emerge. You will allow God to create His masterpiece. And the masterpiece will be you. Michelangelo said:

I saw the angel in the marble and carved until I
set him free.

Are you living with zest and enthusiasm, determined to absorb the glory of every moment? Or are you feeling stressed, aimless, even let down by life? We *can* all live passionate, romantic, adventurous lives. But make no mistake about it. There will be struggle. There will be tension. There will be the familiar ache. But life in Jesus Christ and the hope He offers transcends all of it like an eagle soaring over the mountaintops. After all...

We are loved by the God of passion:

- He created relationship.
- He created "being known."
- He created you so He could cherish you and you could enjoy Him.

We are loved by the God of romance:

- He created music.
- He created warm summer nights.
- He created sunsets and starlight.

We are loved by the God of adventure:

- He created the oceans on which we set sail.
- He created the mountains that we strive to climb.
- He created love so we could experience the deepest joy.

Dare to live richly. Passionately. Abundantly. Live a most excellent life in Jesus. God uses all sorts of things to bring us life and build us up—not just spiritual things. He is all around us, in the moments, the people, the surroundings. Talk about creating a great atmosphere! It doesn't get any better than God.

Today is the day that the Lord has made. You don't have to grin and bear it. You don't have to drag yourself out of bed and dread the day. There is so much life awaiting you. His life. Breathe it in. Live like you mean it!

Fill Up on the Finest

But seek first his kingdom and his righteousness, and all these things will be given to you as well.

MATTHEW 6:33

I was at my home away from home—the airport. As always, the baggage-claim area was crowded like an army of ants invading a cookie crumb. I always stand back and let the frenzy calm down before I attempt to find my belongings. As I was waiting and watching, I set my eyes upon a little boy holding his father's hand. I often see a scene like this. There is something about the innocence, the trust, and the abandonment that puts a smile on my face and makes my heart grow warm.

Here was this little fellow with his dad. His eyes were following the same path as his father's. He was totally on a mission to help find their luggage. As I took in the visual delight in that moment, I couldn't miss the gigantic backpack that covered him from the middle of the back of his head all the way to the top of his legs. I chuckled. The sack was composed of see-through netting so everything inside was exposed for all to see. The contents stretched the material to its limits.

I could envision this boy that morning, painstakingly

packing for his trip, wanting to include everything that was precious to him. He wasn't about to leave any of it at home. It was all so terribly important. There were cars and trucks and trains, along with Batman and Spiderman and other superheroes. There were all sorts of rubber and plastic things. He had what he needed for his trip.

As I got into the taxi, I thought about how I am like that little child at the airport. Every day I carry a "backpack." Often it is stuffed with all kinds of things that are inessential—"toys" that may not have any value to my overall spiritual welfare.

All of us carry backpacks—filled with the treasures of our hearts—but how likely are we to remember to keep them filled with things that will meet our deepest needs? How often do we yearn to stuff them with things that have little bearing on what we truly need and what is best for our lives?

- money
- success
- a great face or teeth or body
- a big house
- a nice car

- friends
- a boyfriend

Yes, even...

- a husband
- children
- ministry

That is not to say having these things is bad. But to seek God's kingdom first is the secret to acquiring true riches. God is so kind and loving and full of grace. He is ever so patient with me as I "grow up" and truly understand what I need to make it through life with a heart full of His treasures.

That child at the airport knew his father was going to take care of him, watch out for him. Give him exactly what he needed to feel loved and safe and cared for. There was nothing in that backpack that would help that little boy with any daily need. That was going to be his father's business, and he trusted that his father would provide for him.

The same is true for us. As we mature in life, we can have that same level of trust and innocence and also store up treasures that will last. As Jesus pointed out so poignantly, "What good would it do to get everything you want and lose you, the real you?" (Luke 9:25, MSG).

We were made to worship God and Him alone. If we don't worship Him, we will definitely worship something or someone else. Before we are aware of it, we have given away God's place in our lives. He comes in second, third, or even last place. Usually when we've given His place away, other things move in. Then we wonder why we lose our way or why we live with an unfulfilled heart. The abundant life He offers us is then so far from our reach.

In our affections something else steals His place.

In our addictions something else holds His place.

In our relationships someone else takes His place.

In our desires something else fills His place.

When I was having my house in Nashville built, I learned a lot about "fillers." The stuff is called caulking (you know, that puttylike stuff that builders and handypeople use to fill cracks and repair seals around windows). Whenever there was a dent or a groove or a hole somewhere in my house, I heard, "Well, it just needs a little caulking."

I can't tell you how often I received that answer from the workers. It didn't matter if I pointed to wood or Sheetrock or plastic. "We'll just put some caulking there."

Putty in places that should have been Sheetrock or wood! I was amazed. I kept worrying that with the first big rain my house would go floating away in a massive putty pile! What a nightmare. I could picture myself pointing at this gigantic mudslide and saying, "That's where I used to live."

Fillers don't cut it. Eventually they wear out. They aren't going to hold up for the long haul. When that happens (from our own doing, remember), we get an attitude: *I deserve better than this!*

We become disappointed and angry. We become bitter, sad, and hopeless. We certainly lose our way. Then we want to give up. In this vicious cycle of unbelief, numbness, and hopelessness, the God of impossible things is left on the sidelines of our lives. We crowd God out of first place. And then we find ourselves out shopping again for something that will fill up our empty places. We try to satiate our ravenous hunger with something other than God and the choice "foods" that offer rich and lasting soul-satisfaction.

Eugene Peterson's translation of God's words through the prophet Isaiah gets me every time:

Why do you spend your money on junk food,
　　your hard-earned cash on cotton candy?
Listen to me, listen well: Eat only the best,
　　fill yourself with only the finest.
　　　　(Isaiah 55:2, MSG)

The *New International Version* says it this way:

Why spend money on what is not bread,
　　and your labor on what does not satisfy?
Listen, listen to me, and eat what is good,
　　and your soul will delight in the richest of fare.

My favorite story in Scripture is Mary's anointing of the feet of Jesus. I love it because what she did was daring and passionate and tender, and it exemplifies the soul delighting in the richest of fare. While there was all the hubbub of eating and talking and the celebrating of Jesus and the resurrection of Lazarus, Mary recklessly abandoned herself to her own "fine dining" experience.

> Then Mary took about a pint of pure nard, an
> expensive perfume; she poured it on Jesus' feet
> and wiped his feet with her hair. (John 12:3)

What Mary did was scandalous in that day. In fact, to everyone around, it was shocking, offensive, and grossly improper. It was even passionate, romantic, and adventurous! Oh, how I love it!

She had one pint of pure nard—sixteen ounces of an oily paste that found its way from India to this little house in Bethany. It was potent and extremely costly. You had to dilute it before using it because the scent was so powerful. And here was Mary—her hair let down in public—pouring this priceless, precious nard all over Jesus' feet in a matter of moments. Can you just hear the commotion?

"Dab him with it! Don't—"

"She let her hair down! Immoral!"

"The perfume is being wasted!"

"How undignified!"

If Jesus didn't speak up for her, she would have been utterly shamed, humiliated, and scarred.

"Leave her alone!" (My Italian interpretation: "Shut up!")

He knew that her act was coming from a grateful heart—a transformed heart. In that moment she was selfless. Somehow she knew He was going to die, so she gave all she could—all that was precious to her—because of all she had been given. He canonized her right there on the spot, to the point where she is recorded in Scripture and still spoken of today. Mary gave her relational dowry and financial future away that day. She was saying, *I don't know what my lifetime will hold after this, but I want Jesus and all that He has.* Her reputation was gone, and it didn't matter because what was important to her was what He thought of her.

Her passion for Jesus motivated her to worship Him regardless of what others thought. Her love for Him inspired the romance necessary to serve Him in such a way. She dared to step outside the cultural norm to experience the adventure of connecting with Jesus with reckless abandon.

There is so much white noise in our culture. We overlook opportunities to feast at the feet of Jesus. We don't "fine dine" with Him. There is change and transformation when we meet Him there. I have found that there is little lasting personal transformation when I don't spend that time with Him.

It doesn't have to be intense Bible reading or praying. It can be just sensing His presence and enjoying whatever is pure and lovely. Putting good into our souls and into our ears. Letting it flow in and out of our hearts. I don't think most of us realize how much this means to God. Mary's story teaches me so much about priorities and worship. I must continue to break my riches at His feet if I am to enjoy the sweet flow of *His* riches into and out of my life.

When Mary poured that perfume on Jesus' feet, can you imagine how strong the scent was, if even one ounce would have permeated the whole room? It gives me goose bumps to realize that the scent more than likely didn't go away with the dinner that day. That scent must have stayed on Him and with Him. When they pressed those thorns into His head, the scent of Mary's worship came out. When the guards beat Him mercilessly, the scent of Mary's worship came out. Even the empty tomb must have had the scent of Mary's worship. Was it important to God? Absolutely. The scent of her worship was there at His darkest moment, and it was there at His most glorious.

Our time with Him—our adoration and worship deeply moves the heart of God. The scent of our worship stays with Him always. Whenever I hear the beloved Christmas carol "O Come, All Ye Faithful," I can't help but lift my face toward heaven…

O come, let us adore Him.
O come, let us adore Him.

It is so easy to lift my hands in worship when I sing this song. It really does make me want to give all to God and to give Him the praises He is due. But I yearn for the adoration to go way beyond the singing. I wonder what my life would really look like if I adored Him with the very breath I take? What if I adored Him with my speech and my thinking, with my actions and in my relationships? It gets tiring putting on different hats and faces and clothes. My goal is to be who I am, where I am, so that hopefully the public and private me will meld into one consistent person.

I want to be that person, living la dolce vita in an ongoing covenant with God. The Israelites made it through the wilderness to the Promised Land to enter into a covenant with God that would sustain them forever, just as the manna from heaven He rained down on them in the desert had sustained them day after day. "This day I call heaven and earth as witnesses against you," Moses exhorted them, "that I have set before you life and death, blessings and curses. Now choose life, so that you and your children may live and that you may love the LORD your God, listen to his voice, and hold fast to him. For the LORD is your life" (Deuteronomy 30:19-20).

Choosing life and not death. It's an everyday choice. There are many days I don't want to deal with choices. But choices affect the quality of my spiritual journey. My choices either bring me nearer to Him and His blessings or take me farther away from Him and His purposes.

Today is the day you can choose life over death. You can get up! Don't stay where you are. Don't postpone living.

Happiness is based on happenings; joy is based on eternal perspective. We can't place our joy and security in something that changes. The good news is that God never changes and His love is constant.

My heart grows weary often. At times I can see depression approaching like a storm rolling in. I can even see my countenance changing. My face and spirit can show easily what my heart is feeling if I don't put on the biggest Oscar act of a lifetime. I'm glad I'm a poor actress; I can't even fool myself for long. I have to deal with my stuff or I can't live with myself. It becomes all too tragic to pretend.

I usually try to get still long enough to see how I got there. Now, sometimes it is simply the awareness of the ache I mentioned at the beginning of this book. You know, just being here and not being home. But often I can trace where I let darkness overrule the light. Most of the time it comes back to my choices. What did I let into my soul? Did I believe a lie? Did I let go of God's hand?

There is so much we have access to now through the Internet, through the movies, and through the media. I can easily pollute the rivers of God's life in me by what I read and watch and participate in. I don't want to stick my head in the sand and be holier than thou. That would be pointless, useless, and arrogant. But I do want to find the balance of what Scripture says about being in the world but not of the world. There is a reason for that. We are weak in our flesh. Our senses cause us to get carried away in the moment. We lust and crave. I love what Sarah Groves sings so poignantly:

Eve was the first but she wasn't the last

But I can choose God. I can choose life. Most of the time I can be in charge of what I allow to saturate my soul. You've heard the phrase "Garbage in, garbage out." I have also found this to be true: "Garbage in, garbage stays in." I get discouraged. I doubt. I gossip. I grow bitter. I get angry. Creepy, crawly, ugly things make their way into my soul, and I feel infested with the very things that squeeze the life out of me. His life. Then it all tumbles like a stack of dominoes, and I wonder why I can't hear God. I sometimes even question if He is there.

I am learning to remember what I feel like when I let myself get to that state. It's like how I've kept my weight down since I lost thirty pounds many years ago. I love the quote, "Nothing tastes as good as being thin feels." I remember the weight and how much I hated being there. I hated it enough to continue to try to live differently and make healthier food choices. Now I try to remember how much I hate the ugly things that separate me from God's presence so that I make healthier life choices.

The book of Matthew includes a heartstopping illustration of our power to choose. Jesus had been arrested, and it was the governor's custom to release a prisoner chosen by the crowd. The other prisoner was Barabbas, a murderer who had taken part in a rebellion against the Roman government.

"Which of the two do you want me to release to you?" asked the governor.

"Barabbas," they answered. [In the book of John, it says, "Give us Barabbas!"]

"What shall I do, then, with Jesus who is called Christ?" Pilate asked.

They all answered, "Crucify him!"

"Why? What crime has he committed?" asked Pilate.

But they shouted all the louder, "Crucify him!"

When Pilate saw that he was getting nowhere, but that instead an uproar was starting, he took water and washed his hands in front of the crowd. "I am innocent of this man's blood," he said. "It is your responsibility!"

All the people answered, "Let his blood be on us and on our children!"

Then he released Barabbas to them. But he had Jesus flogged, and handed him over to be crucified. (Matthew 27:21-26)

Think about this scene. It must have been something…the shouting…the pointing…the demand! If you had been there, what do you think you would have chanted? Jesus or Barabbas? When I first thought about it for myself, I knew I'd have picked Jesus. Of course I would've picked Jesus. Well…I hope I would've picked Jesus.

Give me Jesus! Give me Jesus!

But then I kind of meditated on the text a bit. I thought about my everyday choices. I thought about the attitude of my heart. What are my choices? What do I ask for now? I came to some unsettling conclusions. What I deal with—what we all deal with—is much more subtle than "Give me Barabbas." We say "Give me!" all the time, but we often ask for something other than Jesus. The crowd in the ancient courtyard had a choice. They chose Barabbas. We have a choice. What do we choose? What do we reach for to satisfy our taste for passion, romance, and adventure?

You see, we *want* all the time. It hasn't changed since the Garden of Eden. In that glorious state of God's provision for man and woman there was still a wanting more, a taste for something else. Almighty God said to eat of the Tree of Life, but they chose to eat from the tree that brought death.

Adam and Eve gave God's place away.

Solomon gave God's place away.

David…Peter…you and me.

- Give me…a husband.
- Give me…a changed husband.
- Give me…a new relationship.
- Give me…the career I want.
- Give me…the body I want.
- Give me…the money I want.
- Give me…the happiness I want.

We are often as impatient as a child at a candy counter. With hardly a pause we take matters into our own hands. We tend to doubt God as our life-giver. We tend to feel like God is holding back from us. We feel like we are missing out on something. We feel shortchanged. And you know what? Those things that aren't from the Lord's hand become fillers for what He truly wants us to have. All too soon we find ourselves more lonely and empty than before we filled up on other things. We don't want to deny ourselves. So I have written for myself a Do Not Deny list:

- Do not deny yourself the life that God yearns to give to you.
- Do not deny yourself His blessing.
- Do not deny yourself His best.
- Do not deny yourself access to all that He is.
- Do not deny yourself the hope of a new day.

We can easily block the blessing. I am just as guilty as anyone of having a too-busy life. Things *must* get done. They cannot wait. We have become people who look intact, but in reality the stress is killing us and the tapestry of our lives is becoming tattered and slowly unraveled. I have a perpetual to-do list. If I am not writing it down,

I am thinking about it. The list occupies my mind and takes some of my sleep away. I am embarrassed to say that even sometimes during a sermon at church, I am writing away about what needs to be accomplished later. I often have to go before God to get refocused and gain perspective on how out of whack my life has become. I am then able to shift my to-do list to a to-be list:

- Be still.
- Be willing.
- Be quiet.
- Be patient.
- Be in God's company.

When I first heard that Mel Gibson was doing a movie about Christ, I was a little skeptical. There have been many different versions of "the gospel" from Hollywood in recent years. But before long I was reading about *The Passion of the Christ* in magazines and hearing Mel being interviewed, and I was quickly convinced and impressed and knew it was the real deal. It was truly going to be about the Jesus of the Holy Scriptures. He spoke of it all with reverence and conviction. It was going to be full-fledged agony and passion on-screen. Not to sensationalize but to show a historical picture. Not for gore but for the glory of God.

So many different moments from the movie pierced my core, but I'd like to relay just one portion of that great masterpiece. It has stayed with me and has affected my journey with Jesus in a powerful, daily way.

If you haven't seen the movie, it won't be hard to envision this one scene with me. The essence of what Scripture says is there. Of course, Mel Gibson took some artistic liberties in conversation but nothing that one couldn't imagine hearing.

Jesus has just been beaten and tortured with such force that it's hard to keep looking at His bloodied, torn body. He is trudging down the streets toward Golgotha dragging a gigantic wooden cross. The pathway is packed with people, and Mary and John are being pushed and shoved some length behind Him amid the crowd. Mary turns to John in the chaos and says, "Help me get near Him."

John immediately takes her arm and pulls her over to

the side, behind a stone wall, where she runs forward through a side passage. In an archway, she catches her breath and leans her body flat against the wall as she hesitantly peers around the corner. Oh, how frightening to see her son in the grip of torture and mockery. The moment would need grace and courage.

She runs to meet Him as He falls to the ground. She reaches for Him. Just then, a flashback of when He was a little boy fills the screen. The little Jesus falls and she runs to bring Him comfort and assurance. Here now is her baby boy. Bruised and broken.

How could she ever have imagined what she would live through when the angel told her years before that she would conceive the Savior of the world? She can't save Him, but He is about to save her and all of mankind. She can't go in His place because He is about to take hers.

Mary and Jesus are face to face, and He strains to make eye contact with her. One eye is swollen shut and the other is barely open. Still, He looks at her and speaks words as only God can speak: "See, Mother, I make all things new."

When I heard Mary ask John to help her get near Jesus, it quickened the longings in my own heart. I want that to be the cry of my soul—that I will live my life getting near Him.

A friend in Nashville recently lost her dear husband. He had a heart attack in his truck as he was pulling up the driveway at the end of the day. John was a big guy who would fall under the gentle-giant category. I had known Shirley years ago. Since then I had moved back to New York but had heard that she had changed so much. She is a brilliant woman, but her countenance often used to be cold and her posture toward those around her presented a wall of protection. I was sweetly surprised to hear how soft she had become. The words *kind* and *humble* were now used to describe her.

When I went to the service for John, I waited in line with hundreds of others to share my sympathy with Shirley. When I got close to her, we embraced. She looked at me and whispered through tears, "You know, Kathy, John loved me for so long that I finally started to believe it."

Those words fell directly into my heart. John's love

for Shirley changed her. It rubbed off on her. She softened. She believed. She became alive and new.

It can be the same for you and me.

To have a great relationship with anyone, you must "get near" and spend time. Quality time. Jesus spent an enormous amount of time with His disciples. He wanted to bring them from death to life, to do an extreme makeover on their souls, to make all things new. He wants the same for you and me. As we get near Him and fill up on the finest He has to offer, change will happen. Transformation will take place. The love of God will overwhelm us and make us new. We'll become makeover miracles.

Keep Your Life Web Free

When we choose deliberately to obey him,
then he will tax the remotest star and the last
grain of sand to assist us with all his almighty
power.

OSWALD CHAMBERS
My Utmost for His Highest

When I first encountered Rosie, I thought she looked like a bear…and bears can eat you. But I have come to love her and even let her slobber on me whenever she feels inclined. If my manager's New-foundland barks or runs with fervor in my direction, I can still get a shiver up my spine in anticipation of losing a limb. But she always reassures me that she just wants to love on me.

I was tickled by Rosie's presence during the course of a recent dining experience. While Matt and his wife, Deb, and five guests enjoyed delicious, gourmet food from a table that was regally set, I found myself repeatedly knocking my feet into some part of Rosie's body, which was sprawled partially under the table, where she could be near the comforting hum of friendly conversation. Her belly showed and her paws rested in the air above her. (She is oblivious to and unashamed of her size.) Everyone on her side of the table had to climb over her whenever they needed something from the kitchen. I smiled every time I looked down at her, bumped into her, or clambered over her.

A dog's life—how sweet it is. Dogs eat, sleep, drink, run around, and play. They get hugged and petted and squeezed and cooed over. Then they eat, drink, and sleep some more.

I could really get into that way of life. Especially on the days when I wake up and just know it's going to be one of those days. Before I even put my feet on the floor, I am already feeling weary and overwhelmed. I don't want to be grown up and responsible. I want to run wild and free, and I'm not always sure what that would involve. The pressures of life mount up, and I feel like taking shelter under the covers. I want to lie down, get up to eat something yummy, and then lie down again. Just like Rosie. Maybe someone could coo over me and hug me and squeeze me and tell me how cute I am.

After all, I know what's best for my life and, doggone it, I'm going to go out there and be happy. I mean the goal is to be happy, right? It's my life, isn't it? The voice of God in my spirit when I'm in that state of mind is unmistakable: *Your goal for you is to be happy. My goal for you is to be Mine.*

Much to my delight, I've discovered that the goals are not mutually exclusive. When I truly belong to Him—mind, body, and soul—I possess a joy inextinguishable. But I've had to learn that the hard way.

Oh, what a tangled web I can weave.

- *I know this man is good for me.*
- *I know this friendship is of God.*
- *If I go there, I will be okay.*
- *I can afford it.*
- *It feels like the right thing.*
- *Surely this ministry is what God wants me to give myself to.*
- *I can handle the extra busyness and pressure.*
- *This opportunity must be God's will or it wouldn't have come my way.*

What do I really know? I see through fogged glasses. I think with a self-justifying mind. I feel within human flesh and blood and ego. I love with a conditional heart. God's ways are so much higher than mine.

I have caused more harm than good when I have pursued my own version of happiness. There have been more times than I want to admit when God has saved me from myself, and other times when I've hurt myself and others deeply.

In the past several years of my life, the focus of my Christian journey has shifted and the landscape has taken on a different look. For many years God had to operate like Smokey Bear in my life. His sole job was to keep putting out fires. I didn't give Him room or time to be Lord. In my quest to live big, I have made big messes. I think the reason is that age-old truth: someone's best qualities can also be their worst when used in the wrong way.

For example, I am open and vulnerable by nature. I speak my mind and share my heart very naturally. There are many people who don't live that way. So when I was just being me—at level ten on the being-open scale—it was easy for others to think there was intimacy between us. Sometimes people have been hurt, thinking we were closer than we were. It took a lot for them to open up in the same way. Add to that my huge, gaping hole of needing to be loved and wanted. Charm and talent went a long way, and I am sorry to say that I have contributed to many casualties along the road.

I still pray for God's grace and healing for many of those relationships. Through prayer, studying Scripture, and counsel from dear, honest friends, I was able to see that I was doing life and relationships on my terms. I was hurting others from my broken places, and I was paying the consequences.

I am still in the fixing stage of some of my messes (aren't we all?), but I can truly say that He has changed my heart in some important ways. As the psalmist wrote, "Before I was afflicted I went astray, but now I obey your word" (Psalm 119:67). In other words, as David says a few verses later, "It was *good* for me to be afflicted *so that* I might learn your decrees" (119:71).

It was as if I was living as close to the edge as possible, and I could hear God's voice in the distance but ignored it. When I allowed the Lord to stop being Smokey Bear and tried to listen more and act on His counsel, things started to change. I watched myself and slowly redirected my way of thinking and relating. Now I am more careful in my sharing. I try to be sensitive with my questions. I remember the fallout of relating without God at the helm—having His discernment and wisdom. I by no means squelch my personality, but my goal is to give off the aroma of Christ rather than the stench of my selfishness and manipulation. It has truly changed me. I can honestly say that now I crave God more than anything or anyone else.

- Would I love to feel the pleasure of a night of lovemaking?
- Would I love to live with a reckless ease, as my friend Allyson calls it, eating and drinking and consuming with my eyes and ears to my heart's content?
- Would I love to have my day in court when someone has wronged me or talked badly about me?
- Would I love to never have to watch my words?

The answer to all is yes. But what is natural for me is not necessarily natural to God. What seems fine and dandy in the moment can have long-lasting consequences. Short gain and long pain. The devastation to my own soul is enormous, not to mention the obvious impact on the people around me. That quenching of the Spirit of God is real. You lose your way. You tune out the voice of God's guidance. There is another kingdom in your heart. It revolves around you and not God. That is where the major trouble lies. It's almost as if the life of God in you becomes null and void. You may end up satisfying your need, but you can become pretty useless to others in the process.

Oh, that we would love His ways! They give us freedom.

> I have chosen the way of truth;
>> I have set my heart on your laws.
> I hold fast to your statutes, O LORD;
>> do not let me be put to shame.
> I run in the path of your commands,
>> for you have set my heart free.
>> (Psalm 119:30-32)

Freedom in God's commands? How can there be freedom within the boundaries of His narrow way? Because without the boundaries God sets down for us in Scripture, we are headed for destruction and death. Without lines on every road and highway in America, there would be utter chaos. Without guardrails on bridges and mountain passes, there would be constant casualties. The kingdom of God is set up the same way.

I love the verse, "It is for freedom that Christ has set us free" (Galatians 5:1). I don't think we realize how much baggage we carry around every day. We're weighed down. Chains of all sorts have wrapped themselves around our hearts and minds. We remain locked in our prisons until we let Jesus set us free. Free to be all we are meant to be. Free to love and free to feel. Free to think and free to do. Free to live! Truly live! Is an eagle free to fly? Yes. But not free to swim. Is a whale free to swim? Yes. But not free to fly. Freedom is doing what we were made to do. We can find this kind of freedom only by living within the boundaries God has established for the beloved creatures He has made.

"Be holy, because I am holy," God said. This admonition isn't just for Mother Teresa or Billy Graham. It is for each of us. Through the years, God has shown me gently, yet sternly, the ways that I have walked quite a distance from holiness and settled into mediocre Christian living. You know: "Yes, I love God. He is full of grace. I want to please Him. But the church is too strict and judgmental." All that stuff. When we neglect the "holy" command, we revert to being nonchalant or insincere in our pursuit of God's highest and best for us. We make messes and ultimately get to the point where we don't even care anymore. It all should come back to this:

- *Lord, let me hear from You.*
- *What do You want me to say—and not say?*
- *What do You want me to do?*
- *How do You want me to live?*

It is said that when the theologian G. K. Chesterton was asked to write a letter to the London *Times* on "What's Wrong with the World?" he wrote back, "Dear sirs, I am."

I have noticed that the people who are the most spiritually evolved are the people who have humbled themselves before a holy and merciful God. In humility there is power because you are teachable enough to hear God and go to higher places with Him. To embrace humility is to experience His strength and enjoy His freedom.

Jesus lived freely in absolute submission to God. I am not particularly fond of words like *submit* (cease resistance, yield) and *submissive* (humble, obedient). Most of us aren't. We don't want to submit. We want to resist. We want our lives to become easier.

But when we do what God says to do, there is sweet freedom. The psalmist proclaims, "The boundary lines have fallen for me in pleasant places; surely I have a delightful inheritance" (Psalm 16:6). *Pleasant* places. A *delightful* inheritance. Do those words sound like they come from a passionless, kill-joy God?

> How sweet are your words to my taste,
> > sweeter than honey to my mouth!
> I gain understanding from your precepts;
> > therefore I hate every wrong path.
> Your word is a lamp to my feet
> > and a light for my path. (Psalm 119:103-105)

Oh, that we would experience God's words of direction and admonition as *sweet* rather than bitter. Naturally, we want what is pleasant to *us*. What brings *us* pleasure. What makes *us* comfortable. But we lack His supernatural wisdom. "There is a way that seems right to a man, but in the end it leads to death" (Proverbs 14:12).

Many times what we are so sure will taste delicious and be satisfying is momentary, fleeting, and disappointing. If it is not meant to be and it is not what He can bless, then it will not be life-giving and fulfilling the way we think it will. In fact, it will bring "death"—at least in the form of relational and spiritual disease—to us and to those around us.

I am so great at rationalizing. So many times I've lived in a tense state between could and should:

- what I could do and what I should do
- what I could spend and what I should spend
- what I could eat and what I should eat
- what I could say or what I should say
- what I could think or what I should think

Often I have to get past the waves of my feelings to the truths of God's shoreline. God definitely draws His lines in the sand. He doesn't do it to imprison us but to liberate our souls. That really has been a hard truth for me to grasp. Often when I have seen His lines, I can't wait until the tide rolls in so it can wash them away. But it never does. He never changes, and His truth never changes.

I have learned over and over again that home—a place of comfort, peace, and joy—is being in the will of

God and under *His* covering. I wrote these lyrics in a song called "A Different Road":

> Don't want to live without the peace
> That comes to me when I am by His side
> I've known the freedom there
> Can't find it anywhere
> But in Christ Jesus[1]

The dos and don'ts are hard for a child to hear and understand. We are His children, and His principles can be hard for us. Also, children can't comprehend the love of a parent. But that doesn't stop the parent from expressing it. God adores us. He yearns for us to have His best. He longs for us to live in the light and frolic in freedom. That is abundant life.

> If your law had not been my delight,
>   I would have perished in my affliction.
> I will never forget your precepts,
>   for by them you have preserved my life.
>   (Psalm 119:92-93)

Because I have displayed such expertise at getting tangled, even strangled, by the webs I've been known to weave, allow me to give you some hard-won advice on keeping your life web free:

- No one can be caught in a place that they don't visit.
- "Close to" ends up "captured by."
- Don't be warmed by the fire of sin. Extinguish it.
- Build the kind of memories that you can be alone with tomorrow.
- No one stands toe-to-toe with seduction and survives.

If you are going to fall, fall on the side of His truth. It is safe there. And no one gets hurt. "Great peace have they who love your law," wrote the psalmist, "and nothing can make them stumble" (Psalm 119:165). We have daily opportunities to make choices within the boundaries God has established for us in His Word. It will not be easy. Easy is not the way of the gospel. But He will meet us where the path gets steep and rocky. And to be met by God is an awesome thing.

Temptations will always be there. But so will His grace. Some struggles can be constant. There are those thorns we don't understand. Somehow in the mystery of how God works they are the very things that bring us into His holy presence.

I love this poem, "The Thorn," attributed to Martha Snell Nicholson:

> I stood a mendicant of God before his royal throne
> And begged him for one priceless gift that I could
>   call my own.
> I took the gift from out of his hand, but as I
>   would depart
> I cried, "But Lord! This is a thorn! And it has
>   pierced my heart.
> This is a strange, a hurtful gift which thou has
>   given me."
> He said, "My child, I give good gifts and gave my
>   best to thee."
> I took it home, and though at first the cruel thorn
>   hurt sore,

As long years passed I learned at last to love it
>more and more.
I learned he never gives a thorn without this
>added grace:
He takes the thorn to pin aside the veil that hides
>his face.[2]

Throughout Scripture, God asks something of us so He can *give* something to us (my emphasis added below):

Draw near to God and He will draw near to you. (James 4:8, NASB)

Consecrate yourselves, for tomorrow the LORD will do amazing things among you. (Joshua 3:5)

You will seek me and find me *when you seek me with all your heart.* (Jeremiah 29:13)

The LORD will fight for you *while you keep silent.* (Exodus 14:14, NASB)

Be still, and know that I am God. (Psalm 46:10)

Jesus was a man of sorrows. Acquainted with grief. But Scripture says He was perfect and complete and lacking in nothing. There are aspects of the Lord that we will not see without suffering—whether on our knees like He was in Gethsemane or on the cross like He was at Calvary. In one place His will was decided. In the other it was completed. Finished. We are made whole only in Jesus.

So get all of your webs out before God. He can handle them, and He longs to heal you. You are so valuable to Him. He longs to make all things new in and for you. You don't repair something unless it is valuable. He is the essence of redemption. In our humanness we can feel such self-contempt. But don't concede! Don't give up! No one is unredeemable. No one is unhealable.

The God of passion, romance, and adventure will make the difficult days and times in our lives into a story worth telling. I know that I am more than I ever thought I could be because of Jesus. He has given me the freedom to be the real me. The best me. Not what my family thought I should be or what a record company thought I should be or what a friend thought I should be.

Today I choose to live my life trusting in His words,

listening to His voice, and heeding His convictions. It is hard, but I continually learn that life is full of hard choices, and God honors them. Freedom is worth fighting for. If we can bear the boundaries, they will look beautiful on us—the loss, the loneliness, the hard choices. They will leave beauty marks. I love what C. S. Lewis wrote in *Letters to An American Lady:* "How little people know who think that holiness is dull.… When one meets the real thing, it's irresistible."

> Keep me safe, O God,
>> for in you I take refuge.
>
> I said to the LORD, "You are my Lord;
>> apart from you I have no good thing."…
>
> LORD, you have assigned me my portion
>> and my cup;
>> you have made my lot secure.
> The boundary lines have fallen for me
>> in pleasant places;
>> surely I have a delightful inheritance.

I will praise the LORD, who counsels me;
    even at night my heart instructs me.
I have set the LORD always before me.
    Because he is at my right hand,
    I will not be shaken.

Therefore my heart is glad and my tongue
    rejoices;
    my body also will rest secure,
because you will not abandon me to the grave,
    nor will you let your Holy One see decay.
You have made known to me the path of life;
    you will fill me with joy in your presence,
    with eternal pleasures at your right hand.
    (Psalm 16:1-2,5-11)

Home is in God's will. Peace is living within His boundaries. Pleasure and joy are available in abundance at His right hand. He beckons you to thrive there.

Talk to God

God hears you, and something is happening
whether you see it manifested in your life
now or not. In fact, every time you pray,
you're advancing God's purposes for you.
Without prayer, the full purpose God has
for you can't happen.

STORMIE OMARTIAN
Praying God's Will for Your Life

A couple of years ago, I was traveling on a very small jet. It was the kind with just two seats on either side of the plane. I despise flying, but I must do it every week. I always pat the plane before I step into it: *Keep this baby in the air, Lord.*

I took my seat next to a lovely lady that day. I smiled at her as I reached for something to read. She smiled back. Sometimes people don't smile back. I hate that. After about ten minutes into the flight, it sounded as if the engines of the plane completely shut down. I looked at the lady next to me, and she looked at me. I had goose bumps and was beginning to sweat. She simply raised her eyebrows and continued reading. I kept looking back and forth to see if anyone else thought we were all going to die. Finally, I said, "Can I hold your hand?"

"Sure. First time flying?"

Oh, God. I am embarrassed to tell her.

"Hey, aren't you Kathy Troccoli?"

Yes, I am. I know I look like the biggest scaredy-cat in

the world. *And I probably am. But I promise I love God and trust Him.*

"Yes, I am."

"I love your music. As a matter of fact…"

She was so sweet, but all I heard was, "Blah, blah, blah, yada, yada, yada."

As her mouthed moved I prayed, *Oh, Lord. Don't let me die this way. I mean, I know I ask You a lot to not let me die of cancer or in an elevator and things like that. But please don't let me die going down in this plane.*

All I can tell you is the truth of what my spirit heard next.

"I love you, Darla."

What?

"I love you, Darla. You are going to be okay."

Darla? Darla? Oh no! I am definitely going down! God forgot my name!

Well, needless to say we made it. I let go of that poor woman's hand halfway through the flight and never really did hear a word she said. When I got home I kept thinking about my conversation with God on the plane. I was so confused by it all. I decided to look up the name Darla on an Internet site. It said…

Darling.

I wanted to cry. I am such a sap. He is so tender and even romantic.

He continues to speak to me on different days in different ways. Sometimes it is not what I expect to hear or what I want to hear. Sometimes I have trouble understanding, but He always speaks, and He always opens my eyes when I need to see.

One of the simplest and most enlivening ways my soul celebrates is by talking to God. Who has a relationship with anyone without communicating? I'm convinced that God doesn't want my prayer life to be complicated. There is no need for high and lofty prayer. I don't have to get it right. There is something so safe and inviting about simply talking to the One who knows me best and has my best interest in mind.

I've cried. I've pleaded. I've yelled. I've been silenced. I've listened. Through all the exchanges, I've grown. In *Windows of the Soul,* Ken Gire wrote:

Cultivate my heart, Lord, so I may catch every word that falls from heaven—every syllable of encouragement, every sentence of rebuke, every paragraph of instruction, every page of warning. Help me to catch these words as the soft, fertile soil catches seeds.[1]

On many days, my prayer life consists almost solely of praise and gratitude. I love David's exuberance in Psalm 138. (And remember, this is the same guy who also talked to God from the ends of many ropes and the bottoms of many barrels.)

Thank you! Everything in me says "Thank you!"
    Angels listen as I sing my thanks.
I kneel in worship facing your holy temple
    and say it again: "Thank you!"
Thank you for your love,
    thank you for your faithfulness;
Most holy is your name,
    most holy is your Word.
The moment I called out, you stepped in;
    you made my life large with strength.

When they hear what you have to say, GOD,
all earth's kings will say "Thank you."
They'll sing of what you've done:
"How great the glory of GOD!"
And here's why: GOD, high above, sees far
below;
no matter the distance, he knows everything
about us. (verse 1-6, MSG)

I have known Jesus since 1978, and I am still amazed that I can call on Him anytime, anywhere, anyplace. I don't have to wait until He gets home and listens to His voice mail. I don't have to wonder if He will check His e-mail. I don't have to send Him an overnight delivery. He is ever present. He's there when I call. Listening, loving, and leaning in my direction.

Prayer is not all labor and lament; it is also simply an expression of love and trust and praise. I love the times when I am in my car and feel like He is in the passenger seat right next to me. I just talk. He just listens.

- "I'm worried about this, Lord."
- "I hate that I acted that way. I'm sorry. I can be such a jerk."

- "Please keep my nieces safe. Keep them growing with You. I love them so."
- "I ate too much. I feel gross. Help me get back to some sort of discipline."
- "Where do You want me to be next year as far as singing and speaking go?"
- "Will You help me not to be sad about getting older? I love my forties, Lord, but life is going by so fast. I heard that AARP starts at fifty now. It's kind of freaking me out."
- "Do You think plastic surgery is wrong? I mean, people are saying stuff like, 'Don't you want to be the way God made you?' But, Lord, don't You think people are trying to do just that?"
- "I'm still really hurt by so-and-so. Help me to get over it. Sometimes I want them to hurt like I hurt. I hate that I feel this way."
- "Give me Your hands, Your mind, Your mouth. I want to accomplish Your business today, Lord, not mine. Free me from slavery to my own lusts—overeating, lack of discipline, hopelessness. Rescue me from powerful enemies."
- "Let me have Your heart for people."

- "May my home be a sanctuary of love and life, a harbor for angels."
- "Grant me a reputation based on the love and the heart of You, Jesus."

God nods. He hears. He tells me things. I sense them in my heart. Sometimes I can hear Him chuckle.

Other times I feel His compassion and comfort, like when I am having a hard day or a down day. He shows up in all sorts of ways. Someone may call, and I know their words are exactly what He wants to say to me. I may plop open the Bible, and there is a "kiss from the King"— a word that lets me know that He is hearing the deepest cries of my heart.

Sometimes I can't even get to, much less articulate, what I'm feeling. That's when I know I just need to be still and let the Holy Spirit massage my soul. I am filled with all sorts of emotions, but as my friend Marilyn Meberg says, "Emotions don't have brains." It's like I just need to let whatever is happening in this crazy woman body of mine pass on through.

What is the difference between a Doberman and a woman PMSing?

Lipstick.

I get such a kick out of that because it is so true. Sometimes I just have to pay attention to what may be happening in my hormones. Oh, God is so patient and somehow His supernatural grace has rescued my friends from my tongue.

The challenge for all of us in our relationship with God is finding the "you and me" time we so desperately need in our lives that are overrun with work, family, carpool, ministry, friends, and an endless to-do list. Some days I feel like I don't even have time to brush my teeth. And yet I *need* to make the time to get still. To just "be" with Jesus. To find out who—and whose—I am again.

I am personally amazed that Jesus found the time to be alone with His Father. As He became more and more sought after and tugged on by the crowds, just imagine His predicament. Surely the disciples were all vying for His time and attention. I'll bet He was tired and hungry and stressed much of the time. And He was God! We think *we* want to run away and hide!

All over the Gospels we read that Jesus took breaks from the intensity of His daily life. He went to the mountains to pray. He went *alone* to pray. He was God, but He was a man. He knew that for His own sanity and the preservation of the kingdom of God within Him, He needed to have time alone. He needed to focus and re-group. He needed to get His bearings. And He knew that this would only happen through prayer. How much more do we need to do what He did?

There are consistent times in my life when I know I must hide out with God. I am peopled out. I am tired. My list of priorities gets all screwed up. If I don't start at the top of my list with God trickling down into every-thing else, I end up having everything else without the blessing of God. In other words, if I don't get divine bearings, I start to give out of emptiness and not out of fullness. I am quick to get impatient and angry. I get frus-trated, and I exasperate others and myself.

Over the years I have discovered some really simple things I can do to keep myself talking to God above the noise of everyday life.

I take a drive. I have had some really poignant and powerful times with God when I shut the world out. My surroundings and His creation remind me of how small I am and how big God is.

I listen to instrumental music. It calms my soul, and soon I am in sweet communion with God. There are stirrings in my soul and I know it's Him.

Let it go.

Don't worry.

Say you're sorry.

All He wants to say enters into the doors of my heart, and what I couldn't hear or might just ignore is addressed. I need to shut the world out and let it be just Him and me.

Sometimes I make a conscious effort to get on my knees. It is not that God hears me better there, but somehow my posture helps me to humble myself, get quiet, and be in a position to hear and receive from a Holy God.

When I can't stop the chatter in my own head, I call a friend I trust and ask for prayer. I do this when I know I need to pray but I'm weary. When I am emptied out and don't even know what to pray. When my faith is low.

- Where am I going?
- What am I doing?
- Where are You, Lord?

- I can't hear.
- I can't see.

At those times, I say, "Pray for me. Pray with me." I don't try to go it alone. Just hearing someone pray over me buoys my spirit. It reminds me of the power that goes way beyond my weakness. My soul fills up with hope like a car's empty gas tank being filled at the pump.

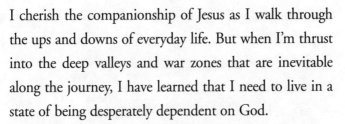

I cherish the companionship of Jesus as I walk through the ups and downs of everyday life. But when I'm thrust into the deep valleys and war zones that are inevitable along the journey, I have learned that I need to live in a state of being desperately dependent on God.

There are some seasons in our lives when we feel like we are in an all-out battle. We feel attacked, afraid, vulnerable, and very small. But when we remember that we are *His,* we can also rest in the fact that what concerns us concerns Him. I love the way the *New American Standard Bible* translates Psalm 138:8:

The LORD will accomplish what concerns me;
Your lovingkindness, O LORD, is everlasting;
Do not forsake the works of Your hands.

The Lord responds with loving attention not only to our daily ups and downs but also to our desperate cries for help.

In 2 Chronicles 20, there is an amazing story that always boosts my faith. Jehoshaphat was the king of Judah. A vast army was going to come against Judah. Without the help of God, it would be complete disaster for the Jews. The king cried out to God in front of all the people:

If calamity comes upon us, whether the sword of judgment, or plague or famine, we…will cry out to you in our distress, and you will hear us and save us. (verse 9)

He goes on to say:

For we have *no power* to face this vast army that is attacking us. We do not know what to do, but our eyes are upon you. (verse 12, emphasis added)

Here is what the Lord said to them:

Do not be afraid or discouraged because of this
vast army. For the battle is *not yours, but God's.* . . .
You will not have to fight this battle. Take up
your positions; stand firm and see the deliverance
the LORD will give you. . . . Do not be afraid; do
not be discouraged. Go out to face them tomorrow, and the LORD will be with you. (verses
15,17, emphasis added)

They went out the next day after worshiping the
Lord and continued to give thanks to Him. The Lord set
up ambushes against the enemy. Yes, and they were
defeated. I love that Scripture says the kingdom of Jehoshaphat was at peace, for his God had given him rest on
every side.

This is relevant to all of us as we battle stresses and
temptations and many different trying situations throughout our days on the earth. It is all about God's power and
not our own. God said to "take up your positions." Stand
firm in obedience and prayer. Let God fight for you
because He never loses. Go out and face tomorrow and

another tomorrow and another tomorrow with confidence that the Lord sees and knows and has a plan for your deliverance. God gave Israel *rest* on every side. He will do the same for us.

> The eyes of the LORD are on the righteous
>> and his ears are attentive to their cry.
>> (Psalm 34:15)

Psalm 34 is one of my favorites. I have held on to its comfort and reassurance through some of the darkest times of my life.

> I will extol the LORD at all times;
>> his praise will always be on my lips.
> My soul will boast in the LORD;
>> let the afflicted hear and rejoice.
> Glorify the LORD with me;
>> let us exalt his name together.

> I sought the LORD, and he answered me;
>> he delivered me from all my fears.

Those who look to him are radiant;
>   their faces are never covered with shame.
This poor man called, and the LORD heard
>>   him;
>   he saved him out of all his troubles.
The angel of the LORD encamps around those
>>   who fear him,
>   and he delivers them.

Taste and see that the LORD is good;
>   blessed is the man who takes refuge in him.
Fear the LORD, you his saints,
>   for those who fear him lack nothing.
The lions may grow weak and hungry,
>   but those who seek the LORD lack no good
>>   thing....

The righteous cry out, and the LORD hears
>>   them;
>   he delivers them from all their troubles.
The LORD is close to the brokenhearted
>   and saves those who are crushed in spirit.

A righteous man may have many troubles,
>   but the LORD delivers him from them all;
he protects all his bones,
>   not one of them will be broken....

The LORD redeems his servants;
>   no one will be condemned who takes refuge
>   in him. (34:1-10,17-20,22)

When we cry out, the Lord *always* hears. He doesn't ever give me a cold shoulder or put me on a guilt trip. There are so many times when I am alone with Him that I am completely myself—just Him and me—with my soul completely naked. Even if I am embarrassed in front of myself, He is not. He is safe. How remarkable.

Dee Brestin and I have written books about being the bride of Christ. To say He "married beneath Himself" when He loved me to Himself is an enormous understatement. I will keep thanking Him forever.

No one has ever truly sought the Lord without finding Him. He can't stop reaching out to us because He is the essence of love. Love can't help but express and communicate itself. Louis Evely wrote:

We obstinately resist God
by hiding under layers of distraction
and indifference,
repugnance and antagonism.
But every desire we have for Him
and every prayer
is like the stroke of a scrub plane
that thins down our wooden-hearted
incredulity;
and when we've prayed enough
and the boards are worn quite through,
we'll realize God was there all the while,
waiting patiently,
pressing hard to set us free.

Prayer alone can wear down our frightful
resistance to God.
Praying is exposing ourselves to His influence,
placing ourselves under His command
so that He may do in us for once
what He'd want to do forever,
giving Him, at last, time and opportunity
to entrust Himself and His secrets to us,

as He's planned from eternity.
Praying is letting Him kill in us
    that boorish, loud-mouthed, egotistic character
        whose bellowing keeps us from convers-
            ing with God.[2]

I remember the days years ago when I was bound by depression. It was like my heart was being strangled but never quite put to death. I would barely utter His name. But He gave me the courage to say it. I loved singing on my worship record that wonderful Gaither song:

Jesus, Jesus, Jesus
There's just something about that name
Master, Savior, Jesus
Like the fragrance after the rain[3]

I have come to cherish it and wear it on that same heart that has been given such a healing release.

The comfort is that He hears *the heart* of our prayers,

and He understands. He doesn't leave us helpless. He hasn't left us alone. He is always looking out for our good. He is so gentle. And when we don't know what to pray, He says that He will pray for us. His Spirit will pray. He just wants us to relinquish all to Him and ask for help. Even if it is, "Have mercy on me."

I can't tell you how many times the Lord has heard those words from me. And He *has* poured out His mercy. I remember taking a walk on the beach with a friend years ago. We were talking and sharing stories about our mothers. She told me that she couldn't picture ever living life without her mother. At that time I talked to my mom daily. Whether good calls or bad ones, we talked. I said that I couldn't imagine life without my mother either.

Years later I was faced with the devastating loss of my mother. God gave me the grace and *did* have mercy on my soul. Ironically, my mom used to say that God would give me grace when I needed it. I have found that He usually doesn't give it to you before you need it. It comes at the very exact moment your heart thinks you can't take any more.

I can relate so well to the prophet Elijah in 1 Kings 19. He had seen the Lord do amazing miracles. He had heard the Lord Almighty speak. Yet he became like a frightened little squirrel when Jezebel, the wife of King Ahab, threatened his life. She worshiped Baal and was angry that her prophets were slaughtered at the encouragement of Elijah. The people had seen the Lord answer Elijah, but the prayers of the prophets of Baal went unanswered. The passage says that Elijah ran for his life. He also prayed that God would take his life.

I am sad to say that I have prayed that same prayer at times. But God is so full of grace. We are so frail and weak, and we can be so cowardly. But the understanding of God is unfathomable. An angel appeared to Elijah to refresh him. It is written that the angel of the Lord came back again after a little while to help him eat and drink because "the journey is too much for [him]" (verse 7).

The only prayer Elijah prayed was that God would take his life. But God always sees the heart of the matter. He waited for Elijah to regain his strength and then showed him how He would go before him. And He did. God knows when the journey is too great for us. We should always remember that it is never too great for Him.

I find it interesting that Elijah ran first and *then* he prayed. Prayer is not necessarily our first response. How often we fret for hours, staying up all night with anxiety, hardly uttering a word to the One who will not only bring us peace but is in control of everything in our lives.

Speaking of staying up all night. Recently I was having all sorts of weird dreams. I am not talking about the ones like I'm still in school and have to take a test. Not the kind where you keep running but you can never get anywhere. Not even the ones where I find a bathroom just in the nick of time (I was a major bedwetter). These were hurtful dreams that involved people in my past. I had such angst in these dreams. I would find myself reflecting on them during the day. They affected my mood. This dark cloud hung over me until I went to bed. Then I might have the dream again in a couple of days only with a different scenario. I couldn't shake the emotions that came with it.

I kept ruminating over it before it dawned on me that I hadn't asked God to protect me and take it away. When I did—He did—that very night. Now when these kinds of dreams sneak up on me, I immediately give them to Him.

I always find myself again or get my bearings when I let Him in. Especially when I let His Spirit have access to my emotions and my mind immediately. I am even learning to stop and pray on the spot when someone asks me to pray about something. I pray right then and there. James 1:5 says, "If any of you lacks wisdom, let him ask of God, who gives to all liberally and without reproach, and it will be given to him" (NKJV).

We may not understand all the mysteries about prayer. There will be hundreds more books written on the subject, I am sure. But three words say it simply and profoundly. *Talk to God.* Jesus did, and we must also. When I first read in Revelation 5:8 that in heaven there will be golden bowls of incense that are full of the prayers of the saints, I knew it was sacred and serious. Holy and healing. May you and I fill those bowls to overflowing. I know we will marvel in awe and praise when we get there. How precious to Him are the prayers of His people.

Stay Ripe
for the Picking

I don't know what your destiny will be, but
one thing I know, the only ones among you
who will be really happy are those who have
sought and found how to serve.

ALBERT SCHWEITZER

My family moved out to Suffolk County, Long Island, when I was three years old, but I was born in Brooklyn. Even as a toddler I remember thinking how different the open space of this huge island was. There was so much room for me to play with my cousins.

Back in the sixties, Long Island was still populated with many horse lovers. There were fields and farms. There were tiny bungalows by the ocean. I still can smell the salt air and hear the rooster that lived on the Rigbys' farm down the road.

In Brooklyn, the houses were close together. We played on backyards of concrete. It was noisy. There were always lots of people around. Because I was so young, I don't remember many details, but I do remember the peach tree...

The garages were separate from the houses. The concrete driveways would go from the street all the way back to the garage. Some yards had a side area of dirt the length of the backyard. It was only about three feet wide, but that was a lot. People were proud of those tiny gardens they planted in this strip. Tomatoes or basil were usually the choice "crops." We lived upstairs in Grandpa and Grandma Esposito's house.

Grandma managed to grow something quite different than her Italian neighbors did: a peach tree. Yes, a peach tree. And not just a little delicate one either. The trunk of this tree took the whole width of the dirt patch. It soared so high that the branches stretched over part of the neighbor's yard and halfway over ours. I remember standing under that tree and looking up under an umbrella of peaches. I would beg my grandma to pick some even when they weren't quite ripe enough. Even the rock-hard ones were yummy to me. When they were perfectly ripe, she would put them in bushel baskets. There were always enough to give away to the whole neighborhood.

Other folks probably enjoyed peach cobbler, pie, and marmalade from our harvest. But my grandma had a different delicacy in mind. She cut up the peaches and put them in Mason jars. Then she would fill them to the brim with red wine and stack them in the kitchen cabinets. I don't know how long she would let them soak before they were opened, but I know the adults were thrilled when they were.

Talk about a tree growing in Brooklyn. This peach tree was not a tree planted by streams of water. It barely had enough room to grow. And yet it flourished, producing more fruit than anyone could have expected.

If you looked in a manual on how and where to grow a peach tree, I don't believe it would say, "The first thing you need to do is find a small portion of dirt surrounded by concrete in the middle of Brooklyn, New York." But that tree was as healthy and beautiful and fruitful as any peach tree could be. It was a delight to all who set their eyes upon it. What a surprise!

I want to be that kind of surprise to the people around me. I long to represent the character of Jesus in a world that doesn't expect to see the beauty of His character. Jesus bloomed wherever God sent Him. He exuded such extraordinary radiance and power. He did the unexpected. He did it when He spoke to the heart of the woman at the well. He did it when He bent down and drew in the sand and challenged the stoning of an adulterous woman. He even waited three days to come and see His dear friend Lazarus after He was told the shocking news that he was dead. When He was before Pontius Pilate, He could have blown all of His accusers to smithereens, yet He chose to remain silent. Fruit fell off of Him, and those who were hungry ate.

We can follow in Christ's footsteps. Our mercy can be surprising. Our patience can be surprising. Our courage can be surprising—as surprising as a peach tree thriving in a small patch of Brooklyn soil.

I am particularly moved by the surprise of kindness in a world where so many people are predictably rude, indifferent, even cruel. Emerson said, "You cannot do a kindness too soon, for you never know how soon it will be too late."

There are some days where I feel deflated and flat. When I am over it, I can see more rationally and laugh at myself. But when I am in it, this is all I can see:

- *I am worthless.*
- *Who really loves me?*
- *Am I making a difference?*
- *Troccoli, you are a big fat hypocrite!*

The self-denigration goes on and on and can get really ugly. Then one of my good friends will happen to call and notice the discouragement in my voice.

"Something wrong, Kath?"

"Oh…you know…hard day."

I love that there are women in my life who *really* know me. They go right to the heart of what I need. All of a sudden, words of life pour out of their mouth and I find life coming back to me.

Often I will come home off the road tired and drained. I love the feeling of that first moment when I step foot back into "Gracie Manor" (the name I affectionately call my home). She is my peace and my sanctuary. The Lord has been so gracious to me. But there are times when I have awakened the next morning after a huge, powerful event only to find myself a little disoriented—a sort of "out of place" feeling. These are the things that invade my brain:

- *What is it all about anyway?*
- *Who do I belong to?*
- *Maybe I should just hang it up and open an antique store.*

I was having one of those mornings recently when the phone rang. It was Allyson. We have been the best of friends for twenty-three years. She and my friend Ellie are like cornerstones in my life. Through the wind and the rain, they have remained standing and I have taken shelter in their love and their wisdom.

"Hi Coli," she said. "What are you up to?"

"Just making some coffee."

"What's wrong?"

"What do you mean?"

"You sound funny."

"I do?"

"Yes. Are you sad today?"

Ugh. She sees right through me, I realized. "Yeah. A little."

"Oh, Coli. It's okay. It's so normal to feel weary."

"Yeah." Somehow the word *normal* always makes me feel better.

"Don't beat yourself up. You know how easy it is to get attacked when you have ministered to others."

"I know."

"Besides, Coli, remember we are *not* in the garden."

I chuckled. Allyson always says this to me because she knows I want life to work on my terms. No pain. Just peace.

"You are exactly where you need to be. And you are so loved."

"Thanks. I love you too."

Oh, the power of words! May we use them wisely. God's love and His words are so redeeming. Ours can be too, because He lives in us.

There is also a holy comfort in silence, and I believe we need to practice that more. Some questions don't have answers. Only God knows. Some situations just need a graceful ear and a hand to hold. But most of us can be more aware of using our words in ways that will breathe life into those around us. God gives us plenty of opportunities. Don't miss them. Listen to author Christopher Morley:

> If we discovered that we had only five minutes left
> to say all that we wanted to say, every telephone
> would be occupied by people calling other people
> to stammer that they loved them.

Sometimes we feel like our lives are insignificant. You may feel your reach is limited and that your turf is too small. But with Jesus, the goal is to bloom in Him. Then He can use you wherever you are planted. No place is insignificant to the Lord. He is a God who pursues the souls of His creation. He woos constantly. And He wants to use you. God wants you to find your own voice and speak with that voice. Your place in this world has been given to you by God. Delight His soul by flourishing in that place.

In all my travels, I still find Tennessee to be one of the most beautiful states. Living here now, I witness firsthand the lushness of the greenery. There are certain roads that I look forward to driving on just because I know the scenery will exhilarate my soul. Sometimes I think God likes to play show and tell with His creation. Who wouldn't want to show it off? It is rich and full of splendor. It has character and has weathered many storms. Yet it has survived—and survived with beauty and grace.

I love to meditate on the first three verses of Psalm 1:

Blessed is the man
> who does not walk in the counsel of the
> > wicked

or stand in the way of sinners
>   or sit in the seat of mockers.
But his delight is in the law of the LORD,
>   and on his law he meditates day and night.
He is like a tree planted by streams of water,
>   which yields its fruit in season
and whose leaf does not wither.
>   Whatever he does prospers.

Eugene Peterson's translation of the same verses in *The Message* particularly delights me.

How well God must like you—
>   you don't hang out at Sin Saloon,
>   you don't slink along Dead-End Road,
>   you don't go to Smart-Mouth College.

Instead you thrill to GOD's Word,
>   you chew on Scripture day and night.
You're a tree replanted in Eden,
>   bearing fresh fruit every month,
Never dropping a leaf,
>   always in blossom.

I want to be a Psalm 1 woman. Living. Growing. Thriving. Bearing much fruit. A tree planted in a place where nourishment abounds. Yielding nourishment at just the right time, never withering but always blossoming. Radiant. Rich. Powerful. I pray that God can use me for show and tell before the world. According to the writer H. Jackson Brown,

> Good character is more to be praised than outstanding talent. Most talents are, to some extent, a gift. Good character, by contrast, is not given to us. We have to build it, piece by piece—by thought, choice, courage and determination.

Wherever you are, what does your attitude say? What does your countenance say? We have the life of Jesus Christ in our hearts and could serve the richest of fare on a platter to a hungry world. We can be a feast for someone's soul. It makes me sad to see that often we are more concerned with our reputation than His reputation in us.

Father Richard Bass said, "Some are more concerned that they be noticed than that Christ might be seen." Paul wrote to the early Christians in Galatia:

> But what happens when we live God's way? He brings gifts into our lives, much the same way that fruit appears in an orchard—things like affection for others, exuberance about life, serenity. We develop a willingness to stick with things, a sense of compassion in the heart, and a conviction that a basic holiness permeates things and people. We find ourselves involved in loyal commitments, not needing to force our way in life, able to marshal and direct our energies wisely." (Galatians 5:22-23, MSG)

Whenever I put myself under Christ's teaching and wisdom and light, I can't help but bow my head in humble worship. I want to stay ripe for the picking—filled with so much of God that there is a vast array of fruit for people to feast on.

I look forward to spending time with certain people just because they are the real deal, and I know I'll be fed.

I had a very sweet affection for Vestal Goodman. She was one of the most popular southern-gospel singers of her day. With her distinct voice and look, no one could overlook Vestal when she entered a room. I would run into her from time to time in Nashville, and she always impressed me. She never had an air about her. She was just being herself, and Jesus was so natural in her.

No matter what Vestal was doing and whomever she was with, it was all interrupted when she saw someone she knew. I always felt like I was the most important person in the world when I was around her. She would give me the warmest, biggest hug. She was a large woman, and I would relish the moment of putting my head on her bosom and letting her love on me. It was impossible to feel insecure around her. I have often thought about her since she passed on a few years ago.

There aren't many people like Vestal. I wish there were more, and I hope someday somewhere a young woman will think of me with the same fondness that I carry in my heart for Vestal.

Fruit ripens on the vine, and fruit can also rot on the vine. Make yourself available! Keep your fruit ripe for the picking. It will be picked. There is so much need. People are hungry! He'll use you as much as you will let Him.

I don't believe the Lord spent hours and hours looking for a bush that He could set on fire to get the attention of Moses. As Kay Arthur says, "Any old bush will do." He purchased the right to our life with His life. Let Him use it! He gives lavishly. If we live with open hands He will surely fill them. So often we act like owners instead of stewards. We can get so selfish with our time and our stuff. If He is at the center of our minds and hearts, priorities fall in the order that He desires.

> For where your treasure is, there your heart will
> be also. (Matthew 6:21)

I always check myself with this. What do I value most in life or, for that matter, during a certain season? Where are my desires? What are my dreams?

Paul's first letter to Timothy says:

> Command those who are rich in this present
> world not to be arrogant nor to put their hope

in wealth, which is so uncertain, but to put their hope in God, who richly provides us with everything for our enjoyment. Command them to do good, to be rich in good deeds, and to be generous and willing to share. In this way they will lay up treasure for themselves as a firm foundation for the coming age, so that they may take hold of the life that is truly life. (6:17-19)

How I pray that we all could be rich in good deeds and generosity. Only then will we have life that bears the fruit of God's Spirit, a life in which...

- peace comes from God
- hope comes from God
- joy comes from God
- provision comes from God

We don't have to muster it up. We don't have to manufacture it. We don't have to pretend. It is a life about Him and what concerns Him. It is genuine, and it is heavenly rich.

I have met many singles who tell me they are encouraged by my life. Every time I hear that, it blesses me. I rarely do singles conferences because I don't want to be the poster girl for Christian singles. I'd rather be seen as a healthy, passionate, rich woman amidst a married world.

I did, however, speak to a group of college students recently. I already had my message planned, but the woman in charge whispered to me before I started, "Maybe you could also include something about single-ness. So many of them are so discouraged."

I wanted to say, "Hello? They're *what?* So, a woman who could be their mother is going to *comfort them?*"

Then I got annoyed. It was kind of like a scene from *Lizzie McGuire*. Of course, I knew I couldn't speak these things, but boy were they racing through my mind: *They have so much of life ahead of them. There is so much to do. Why does marriage become the end-all and be-all at nine-teen years old?*

Inside I became like the Cowardly Lion in *The Wiz-ard of Oz*. *"Put 'em up. Put 'em up."*

Well, needless to say, I politely told her that I would say a little something about it. During my talk I addressed the students like this: "I heard that many of you are con-cerned about your singleness. I understand what getting married means to many of you. We are definitely made by God for intimacy, and He has designed us with desires for relationship. Some of us are afraid we will be alone, that we will miss out on the greatest love of life. But let me give you some perspective about God's definition of the highest form of love. I believe that is where our joy and fulfillment will be found. So finish my next phrase…

"Greater love hath no man than to…"

"Lay down his life for his friends," they replied.

"Very good. Yet this is how some of you would have the verse read…

"Greater love hath no man than to…get married."

They all chuckled with nervousness. I knew they understood.

The Lord never made that sacred covenant the end-all be-all of love in this life. That is not what the Bible says. Laying down our lives for Him, for people—for the gospel. Now that is the highest love. Living a generous life. That is a Jesus life.

As a single woman, I have learned a valuable lesson that brings joy and fulfillment to my life. I began this practice with my nieces, Maria and Gina, who are now in their twenties, but I continue to practice it with the children of families I am close to. You can build equity into the lives of other people's children. When they reach an age when they cannot hear their parents, they may be able to hear you because in the early years you were faithful to meet them where they were—playing with them, spending quality time with them, and getting involved in their interests. Not an ancillary aunt who greets them at the door or sits next to them at the dinner table, but someone who truly knows them. This may matter in some really trying days when they are teenagers. You may easily be called upon as a parent interpreter: "Say for me what my child cannot hear from me."

You will have a voice and credibility if you've invested yourself in their lives. They will still need a voice of wisdom when they think their parents are nerds or don't understand them. You will have earned their trust when they were young, and the only reason you can influence them now is because you put in the time to establish a relationship with them.

This is a generous life—a life ripe for the picking. As you invest in the lives of others, you impact eternity. What greater love is there?

Earlier, I mentioned the mission trip I took to South Africa, where I had the privilege of working with Peter and Ann Pretorius, great ambassadors for the gospel. Ann looks like she could be a sister to Jackie Onassis. She is regal and classy, and I found myself hanging on her beautifully accented words throughout my time there.

"Kathy," she said to me one day, "I am so thankful that you can see the needs of the people firsthand. We are all part of His body, yet we forget about the toe or the arm or the leg. It becomes infected and diseased because it is not attended to. Then we wonder why the body of Christ can be so sick."

I just took it all in as she went on. "Do you know that we get bags and bags of old clothes? So much of the clothing is soiled or has holes. And you wouldn't believe the shoes. We get so many shoes without the pair. People send us one shoe. How many one-legged children do you see here? It makes me so sad."

It conveyed to me a powerful realization. So often we don't give from our abundance. We give from what we have no use for. I have learned that God not only looks at what we give but also at what we keep. Why do we hang on so tightly to things that aren't even ours in the first place?

We have been given so much. There is a responsibility that comes along with that. We must make a lifestyle of giving not only with our possessions but also with our actions and our words. The way Jesus gave.

I was driving home one night after having dinner with my friend Lyn. I was anxious to get home. There are plenty of days when I can't wait to put on my pajamas and curl up in my bed. As I was turning onto the ramp to get on the highway, I came upon a beat-up little truck with a raggedly dressed man beside it. He was obviously stranded and looked helpless. I slowed down and opened my window just a bit.

"Need help?" I asked.

"I'm out of gas."

"Are you with someone who has gone to get it?"

"No ma'am."

"Okay, stay here. I'll be back."

I knew there was a gas station a little way up the road. I went in and asked for a container for a gallon of gas and filled it up. As I was driving back I thought, *It's dark. It's late. I am by myself. I am a woman. He could be an ax murderer.*

I called my friend Lyn since I had just left her. Before I said anything, she said that she was just about to call me. I ignored that to tell her my situation. She said that she would stay with me on the phone. She sounded like a cross between a mother hen and a drill sergeant. It felt so comforting.

"Make sure your doors are locked. Put the gas in the back of your Jeep. Pull up and slide your window down just enough so that he can hear you tell him that the gas is in the back. If he does anything weird...*take off!*"

I did just that. And everything went as planned. We hung up. Lyn called back two seconds later. "Remember I said that I was about to call you? I felt very impressed that I was supposed to have you talk to my mom. Would you be okay with that? I want to three-way her into this phone call."

Of course I was fine with it, and as she was dialing, I remembered that Lyn had told me that her mother was ninety-three years old.

"Momma, I have my friend K. T. on the phone. Remember her? She is the one that sings and has a ministry. I have her here on the line."

Mary Lyn has short-term memory loss. I believe she remembered me but didn't really make a solid connection. It didn't matter though. She was so sweet.

"Momma, will you pray for K. T.'s—"

Before Lyn could get the words out, I heard, "Dear Lord…"

And oh, the prayer was perfect. It was filled with words I needed to hear and requests that were exactly suited for my life. I began weeping, but I knew that Mary Lyn did not hear me and had no clue what her kindness meant to me. Jesus just flowed out of her. I got off the phone to collect myself. Lyn called back immediately. She caught me boohooing.

It had been too long since I had heard a mother's blessing in prayer. I had no idea that my soul was so thirsty for it. As I continued to drive home, I was so aware of the gift of giving and the blessing of receiving.

Freely you have received, freely give. (Matthew 10:8)

Jesus came to show us what God looks like. And people see what God is like by looking at us. We can affect the credibility of the gospel. Not the gospel itself, but the way it is perceived.

I make it a practice to ask myself, "Will God delight in what I did with my lifetime? What I said during that lifetime? How I responded or acted?" I want to live a life that delights God's heart. I want to be a radiant expression of the life of Christ.

The tomb is empty. Because of that, our hearts can be filled with the glory of God. We can be like the peach tree growing in Brooklyn. Surprising. Thriving. Blossoming. Plant yourself in Him, and let everyone partake of the fruit that will nourish their hungry souls.

Wait in Expectation

In the morning, O LORD, you hear my voice;

in the morning I lay my requests before you

and wait in expectation.

PSALM 5:3

hen I was a child, I would look forward to watching The Wonderful World of Disney on Sunday nights. I loved listening to the music as the show was beginning. I loved the stories. I loved watching Tinkerbell trail twinkling lights as she flew around my television screen. I remember getting sad every week as the show ended, but I loved when the announcer would say, "Don't go away! Stay tuned for scenes from next week's episode." I would feel excitement and anticipation. I couldn't wait for the next Sunday night.

I want to live out my faith that way. I want to live my life staying tuned to what God will do next, ready and full of anticipation for whatever He allows to happen in this world and in my life. I love this verse in the Old Testament:

> Look at the nations and watch—
>   and be utterly amazed.

For I am going to do something in your days
    that you would not believe,
      even if you were told. (Habakkuk 1:5)

You don't even have to be well studied in Scripture to know about some of the utterly amazing things God has done:

- He parted the Red Sea.
- He flooded the whole earth.
- He painted the first rainbow in the sky.
- He turned water into wine.
- He brought a dead man back to life.
- He rose from the grave.

Many of these events and so many others were even foretold, yet people didn't believe they would come to pass. When they did, people were amazed—just as I have been as I've watched the utterly amazing things He has done in my life. He parted my heart and came in like a flood. The same God who was born into a broken world took up residence in my broken heart. He placed me in His hands and painted a rainbow of hope in my soul. I rose from my deadness.

When He spoke of the kingdom of God, Jesus often

talked about the need for His listeners to become like children. One of the many reasons is because children live with wide-eyed anticipation of life. The littlest thing can delight their souls. Surprises will cause them to giggle and squeal with delight.

When I moved to Nashville, I was excited about building my very own home. I owned a condo on Long Island, but somehow this was different. I spent hours figuring out which extras I needed and could afford. One of the things that I knew was a definite was an alarm system. In New York I'd had one. Being single, a public person, and on the road a lot, it was a no-brainer. Still, when I was in the midst of building, some of my friends would ask…

- "Are you going to be okay, alone in that house?"
- "Do you feel safe?"
- "Should you get a roommate?"

The comments did concern me a little, because I have had some trouble with unwelcome visitors at my front door. But I felt pretty peaceful about my new residence, especially after the alarm system and security lights went in. I even had a button installed in my office that would immediately alert the police if I should ever need them.

One afternoon I heard the doorbell ring. There are

small windows on the side of my front door, so I can usually see who is standing there. It was a tall, handsome policeman.

Hmm, I thought, as I tentatively undid the locks and peered out through a crack no wider than my nose.

"Hi, I'm so-and-so," he said. "I'm building the house right next door to your property. I was wondering if you would allow me to cut down one of your trees. It would help me to be able to put in a swimming pool."

"Oh, okay... Let's see. Why don't you show me which one you're talking about?"

I slipped quickly onto the porch and introduced myself. As we walked, we talked further. It turned out he was moving from out of state with his wife and daughter because he'd been appointed chief of police for Metro Nashville.

I thought, *Hello? Chief of police?! Could You be any sweeter, Lord?*

I asked if I could see his home, and then I walked him through mine. (By that time he knew I had an emergency button in my office.) He gave me his card and cell phone number and told me that he would keep watch over my house whenever I was out of town. He also told me to call him anytime if I needed anything. I was utterly amazed. (Don't go there. He's married.)

God is full of surprises. I have learned to expect to see Him show up in places and people and ways I never could have imagined because that is business as usual for God. He will meet our needs. We can wait in eager expectation of His provision. And yes, sometimes He will come in an astonishing miracle or the sweet gesture of a policeman at your front door. But He knows that our biggest need is for Him—that we may believe and know that He is God.

The famous story of the feeding of the masses on a hill beside the Sea of Galilee is a great example of this. "When Jesus looked up and saw a great crowd coming toward him, he said to Philip, 'Where shall we buy bread for these people to eat?'" The account in John 6 tells us that Jesus asked this only to test His disciple's faith. Jesus already knew what He was going to do, and I can only imagine the delight He took in the opportunity to demonstrate His power and love to five thousand people at one time. The Lord was about to do a miracle that far exceeded what anyone expected. From the five loaves and two fish in one boy's lunch, Jesus fed everyone and still had enough to fill twelve baskets with leftovers.

But Jesus had an even greater lesson in mind. He knew that our wanting miracles will often distract us from trusting in God for what He knows is best for us.

John's gospel goes on to say that the next day, the hungry hordes were looking for Jesus again. He knew they were not coming just to be with Him, and He told them so. They wanted their bellies full again. They wanted to be satisfied with earthly stuff. Jesus said to them, "Do not work for food that spoils, but for food that endures to eternal life, which the Son of Man will give you."

The people asked Him what work God required.

Jesus answered simply, "The work of God is this: to believe in the one he has sent."

They weren't satisfied with that response. In fact, they had the gall to insist He perform another miracle like He had the day before so they could believe in Him. They basically said, "Now what will you do? Moses did this… Our forefathers did this… Those people got bread from heaven to eat." They were like children taunting, "Nah,

nah, nah-nah-nah." They wanted their expectations met.

So Jesus said to them, "I tell you the truth, it is not Moses who has given you the bread from heaven, but it is my Father who gives you the true bread from heaven. For the bread of God is he who comes down from heaven and gives life to the world."

"Sir," they said, "from now on give us this bread."

Jesus declared, "I am the bread of life."

The people were irritated because they wanted bread to put in their mouths again, and here was a lowly carpenter's son claiming to be everything they needed and more! Their irritation turned to grumbling and then to outrage. Even many of Jesus' closest followers turned away from Him for good that day. Who did He think He was?

And here it is. We all still do it. We try to manipulate God into a box, into what we want and expect and think we need. He will exceed our expectations, but He will not always give us what we ask for. What He wants most is to give us Himself so we will never go hungry again.

I can't tell you how many times I have thought about the people I met on my previously mentioned trip to South Africa. The things I witnessed during that time often replay in my mind. I am constantly humbled at how blessed and "rich" I am. So many of us, including myself, can live with ungrateful hearts, oblivious to what is happening beyond our own backyard.

Like many of you, I have seen the footage of big-bellied toddlers and skeletal infants. It is one thing to watch scenes of devastation going on around this planet, and it is another thing to actually be there. I saw firsthand the open cuts and bruises and sores, and smelled the awful effects of being without clean water and a bar of soap. I patted the heads of many red-haired children who got their "carrot tops" from being severely malnourished.

Every day we would travel to different villages to feed hundreds of people. The lines were long, and even with the intense heat they waited anxiously for their share of the hot soup. Some would hand me old water bottles, and my heart would break as I tried to fill them to the brim. I even picked a leaf from a nearby tree and used it as a spoon to serve one little baby. Old rusty pots and filthy plastic bowls were their containers.

When the big barrels of soup were almost empty (they were the size of huge outdoor garbage bins), the children would become frantic. Kids would push each other in order to climb into the barrels—just to get another lick.

On other days we would hand out clothes. We laid them in a tall pile and divided the children and young adults into lines. We would assess their sizes as best as we could and then hand them a bundle. It was like Christmas for them. The looks on their faces were priceless.

I will never forget my experience with one little girl. She must have been two or three years old. Clinging to her mother, the only thing she was wearing was a light pink woolen sweater that was ridiculously too small for her. It was painfully tight around her arms, and the front was barely held together by a button and a thread.

I was so excited to hold up a bright new sweater and show her that it was now hers. Much to my surprise, when I tried to take off that old sweater, she clung even tighter to her mother and pushed me away. I tried again and she started to cry. I couldn't convince her that this was a good thing and that she would be so much happier and more comfortable.

If she could have talked, I sensed what she would have said: "Please don't take the only thing I have. It is all I have known. I don't understand this new thing."

I slid the new sweater under her mother's arm. In time, the little girl would know what I was trying to give her.

When I came back to the States, that little girl remained one of my most vivid images. Her tears affected me deeply, especially because I was longing to give her a good thing.

I think God must feel the same way, longing to give us the new thing, but we get settled in the old. We often say we want to be like Jesus, but we don't want to change! Instead of being wide-eyed with expectation, we remain stagnant. Whether comfortable or miserable, we remain where we are. God offers the gift of a new thing on a new path, and we don't take it or follow it. How often we miss out on His best—His wonderful and perfect best.

These are strong words from the Lord. They are powerful and commanding:

> Be careful, or your hearts will be weighed down
> with dissipation, drunkenness and the anxieties of

life, and that day will close on you unexpectedly like a trap. For it will come upon all those who live on the face of the whole earth. Be always on the watch, and pray that you may be able to escape all that is about to happen, and that you may be able to stand before the Son of Man. (Luke 21:34-36)

In so many places in Scripture, God says,

- *Keep watch.*
- *Stay alert.*
- *Wait...you'll see.*

It is so we won't miss Him. It is so we won't pass the truth by. It is so we will be alert to what He wants us to allow in and what He wants us to send out of our lives.

In Matthew 24, verses 42 and 44, when Jesus was talking about His coming, He said, "Therefore keep *watch....* You also must be *ready.*"

In Luke 12:37-38, He said, "It will be good for those servants whose master finds them *watching* when he comes.... It will be good for those servants whose master finds them *ready.*"

In Ephesians 6:18, Paul, after he talked about putting on the full armor of God, said, "Be *alert* and always keep on praying."

I love what he also said in 1 Thessalonians 5:5-6: "You are all sons of the light and sons of the day. We do not belong to the night or to the darkness. So then, let us not be like others, who are asleep, but let us be *alert* and self-controlled."

The gospel accounts show us one of the most profound moments in Scripture—when Jesus was agonizing in the Garden of Gethsemane. He asked the disciples to pray so that they would not fall into temptation. When He returned to them, they had fallen asleep. He said, "Why are you sleeping? Could you men not keep watch with me for one hour? Get up and pray so that you will not fall into temptation."

He went on to say the all-too-true statement: "The spirit is willing, but the body is weak."

He then went away again to keep praying, only to come back and find them sleeping. He left them there and prayed some more. When He returned, He said, "Are you still sleeping and resting? Look, the hour is near."

As I meditated on this scene for a while, my eyes were

opened to something: the chief priests did come. The Lord had made His peace with the Father and was ready. When Judas betrayed Jesus by kissing Him as a signal to the priests, Jesus said gently and yet with power and resignation, "Friend, do what you came for."

Peter drew his sword and cut off the ear of one of the high priests. Jesus immediately told him to put his sword back in its place and said, "Do you think I cannot call on my Father, and he will at once put at my disposal more than twelve legions of angels? But how then would Scripture be fulfilled that says it must happen this way?"

Jesus was on the alert. Jesus was sober. He was prayed up. Jesus understood the will of the Father. He could walk through this painful situation with a holy confidence and peace although His heart was breaking.

The disciples didn't have that peace or knowledge. And it is not like the Lord hadn't told them many times in different ways. Maybe that is the very reason Peter drew his sword and the Lord reprimanded him. He had been sleeping during the very hours Jesus was beseeching the Father on the most significant act that was about to take place for all of mankind. Maybe Peter and the disciples would have known far deeper in their spirits about the true will of God if they had been more alert to the heart of Jesus—if they had been waiting expectantly for Him to reveal Himself.

I was invited to a barbecue at my friend's house. Peggy has a love for gardening, and she is meticulous about watering, pruning, and weeding. She knows every name of every flower and will tell you just by looking at them what they may need that very moment. I marvel at her gift because I am *not* gifted in this area. I have been the killer of many beautiful plants that have entered my home through the years. Whenever someone is kind enough to send me a gift like that, I can almost hear the poor, pretty, living creature screaming as it is brought into my house, "Don't leave me with her...*please!*"

I walked around Peggy's yard—front and back—as she gave me the tour of her gardens. As we walked back into the house, I remarked about the beautiful white flowers in the pots outside her front door. She said, "Oh, those are fake. I put those there because with the kids there is so much going out and coming in. It's just easier."

I couldn't tell at all. The real and the fake mingled well together. Only a keen eye would know. Only a person familiar enough with the real would be able to discern the fake. So it is with our Christianity. There is a lot of deception out there. There are many ways that a follower of Christ can be thrown off the narrow road. Scripture even says to be wise and discerning because they may even preach another Jesus than the one you know (see 2 Corinthians 11:4).

If instruments in an orchestra were not tuned to each other, they would make an awful noise—not music. It can be the same with God's people. If the church as a whole can stay tuned, it will be a symphony of beautiful music. When we rely on our own judgment, we can quickly become noise that makes the world unable to hear the good news of Jesus Christ. And they will go hungry while we stand by with our basketfuls of bread.

We need His holy wisdom to maneuver our way through this life. How easily we can be deceived into believing we just *know* what is best for us and what will satisfy our yearning for passion, romance, and adventure. God is so much wiser, and His loving plans for us are beyond our wildest imagination.

I've been singing professionally for many years. That may sound glamorous, but with this gift I have journeyed through some really confusing and dark places. I was full of expectations of what I thought I should be and what other people thought I should be. So many years were spent working and reaching and climbing. God is so good to have given me blessings of "loaves and fish" until I could "get it." My real work was to believe in Him—to grow in obedience—so that I would see His glory and be more fulfilled than I ever expected to be.

God had other things in mind for me. The singing was to be the icing on the cake. I would ultimately write and speak of His comfort and healing and love. He would use my story. He was preparing me to exhort and motivate others to go to higher places with Him. He has exceeded my expectations.

People often ask about when I first started singing. I've answered so many times that my response now seems watered down: "My dad heard me singing along with

Carole King's *Tapestry* record. He knocked on my bedroom door and said, 'Hey, that was great. Do that again.' The rest is history."

The longer version is that ever since I was a little girl, I somehow knew I was going to do something in the public eye. When I first started to sing, I mimicked others' singing. I'd pick up a hairbrush, a pencil, a stick— whatever I could find—and make it my microphone. I hammed it up and didn't care who was around. My mom would eventually have me "fake sing" for every single person that walked into our house. Then it did so happen that I fell in love with the *Tapestry* record and sang my heart out along with "So Far Away" and "It's Too Late." My father listened to me and encouraged me. I haven't stopped since.

So began my quest to become a singer. I was a young believer involved in Christian music nationally by the early eighties. Fast-forward to 1992. I left the scene for a while to find myself. My gift was intact, but I was not. I needed to get my roots down deeper in the things of God. Also, I really had a stirring in my gut about what I really wanted to do with my life and my talent.

Maybe I'm a Broadway singer. It would be really great to sing at cabarets in New York City. I would love to open for Tony Bennett. Maybe I belong in pop music.

In the winter of 1992, I was all over mainstream radio with a hit called "Everything Changes." It was a great song, but it didn't really ever feel like me. I was thrust into the limelight of that world for just a little while. My family was so proud. But I was miserable. The song wasn't me, and the places where I was performing weren't me. I could not verbalize that at the time. I just felt so sad. To add to my gloom, everyone thought the song was performed by the pop artist Taylor Dayne. It was originally written for her, and the way it was produced made it all the more "Taylorized."

I began the rat race of touring and performing at dance clubs and every possible dog-and-pony show. I even had some great opportunities on television with Jay Leno and the Beach Boys and other famous artists. But oddly enough, I never seemed to grab the brass ring. In fact, I don't think many people get as close as I did to grabbing the brass ring without the huge stardom that comes along with it. It eluded me. It was like a big flash in the pan that died out as quickly as it began.

Why did You let that happen, Lord? I get this opportunity and I don't even feel like people heard my real voice. My family thinks I am a failure. I got so close with no real payoff. I would rather You had put me in a Holiday Inn lounge somewhere.

Fast-forward ten more years. There is nothing I would rather be doing than what I am doing right now. I was thinking about it the other day as I was singing at a Women of Faith conference. I was sitting on a stool in front of thousands of women singing my heart out. Rich, sweet tones. Hopeful, stirring lyrics. Tears and healing. I am exactly where I am supposed to be. I am a motivator. I am an exhorter. My singing helps me do what I have been created to do. I am finally seeing it clearly.

All my questions from ten years ago are answered. The Lord allowed me to go for it, but He protected me from missing His will for my life.

God is sovereign and has a plan for each of our lives. He has a specific agenda and timing for it all to unfold as we follow Him and watch and wait. He knows what is best for us and what will give our souls the deepest satisfaction. We often want to write our stories, but I am so thankful that He will gently take the pen from our hands and write the best book that could ever be written. His plots are filled with passion, romance, and adventure. There is joy and peace within the lines.

We strive to become successful. What is success anyway? I have met some not-nice people who seem quite successful, but are they really? Oh, that we would all grab hold of the life of Christ. He humbled Himself and died on a cross. Was He successful? Absolutely! It was in His timing and for His glory. And He yearns for the same for you and me.

Maybe you're in a place similar to where I was ten years ago. Maybe you're striving for a self-set goal with all your might, yet the brass ring is beyond your reach. Oh, my friend, don't despair. You are right where God wants you to be—on the way to where He wants you to go.

If you'll seek Him first and lay aside your own agenda, you can expect Him to reveal His life and resurrection power in *who* you are in this life. He will lead you to fulfillment greater than you can imagine and to success greater than the world could ever offer. Stop striving to make it on your own. Expect Him to lead you. Expect His goodness and mercy to overtake you. Expect His provision along the way. Wait in expectation. You'll see.

Be a Desperate Woman

As the deer pants for streams of water,

so my soul pants for you, O God.

My soul thirsts for God, for the living God.

When can I go and meet with God?

PSALM 42:1-2

A friend of mine gave me a card that I cherish. On the front is a little girl lifting her hands, finding pleasure in the rain. The words say something like, just when you think you'll never feel joy again, it slowly seeps back into your soul. I often think about what my life would be like if I didn't know Jesus:

- I would be different.
- My relationships would be different.
- I would "pick" different people.
- I would act differently with them.
- My career would be different.
- I would be singing different songs, in different places, to different people.
- My heart would be different.
- I would express that heart differently.
- I would think differently.
- I would act differently.
- My hope would be different.
- I would have none.

I'll never forget the day when hope came into my heart to stay. When I invited Jesus to dwell within me at the age of twenty, I began a personal relationship with Him that sparked a sense of aliveness in my soul that I had never known.

I quickly learned in the following weeks that Jesus never promised me Disney World. But He did promise that He overcame the world and would walk me through anything. Life wasn't going to get easier, but Jesus would carry the burden of it because He was now carrying me. I would learn to say, along with King David, "Praise be to the Lord, to God our Savior, who daily bears our burdens" (Psalm 68:19).

Do you ever meet people who just ooze negativity? It's as if there is this heavy, dark cloud over their heads ready to burst at any minute.

"How are you doing?"

"Oh, you know. I'm all right I guess."

"How's the family?"

"Oh. You know. Family is family. They're okay, I guess."

"How is work going?"

"Oh, it's a job."

I want to run out of the way so I won't get drenched with the "woe is me" that is about to rain down.

Still, I understand that sense of doom and gloom. When I was a little girl, the ground beneath my feet always felt like it was shifting. I was sure that one day the bottom would fall out and I would be consumed. Most days, I felt like there were ominous clouds hanging over my head. I expected a downpour any minute. Even at a very young age, a sense of oppression and heaviness lodged deep within me. Being surrounded by my boisterous, extended Italian family sometimes only convinced me that something was very wrong with me. My dad would often ask my mother, "Why is Kathleen always crying?"

I must say that most times, there wasn't a specific reason. But the weight of the world was on my shoulders. Life felt sad even amidst the laughter. I seemed to need safety and a shelter from things I couldn't even name. I just hurt.

Because of that, I clung much too tightly to people. I tried to find my identity in all sorts of things. I explored many different philosophies, hoping I would reach some sort of conclusion about the world. At times I felt angst, and aimlessness would consume me.

Even though there is great mystery this side of heaven, I am now certain I will not fall into an abyss and spin round and round in a life that has no meaning. Just knowing that God makes sense of the things that I don't understand takes that weight off of my shoulders and puts it on His. I cling desperately to Him most days of my life. And when I hold on to Him, I hold on to hope.

> Yet this I call to mind
> and therefore I have hope:
>
> Because of the LORD's great love we are
> not consumed,
> for his compassions never fail.
> They are new every morning;
> great is your faithfulness.
> (Lamentations 3:21-23)

So many people take their own lives. Many lose their minds. People cling to their addictions as if they were their best friends. They hide behind walls of secrecy. When I hear the sound of my alarm...

- the only reason I drag myself out of bed is...because He lives.
- the only reason I face the day with any kind of strength is...because He lives.
- the only reason I want to be nice to people is...because He lives.
- the only reason I have sanity in the uncertainty of this crazy world is...because He lives.

I am so grateful that He wooed me to Himself.

I enjoyed a good laugh with an audience recently when I described the pin I would wear if I were to transparently hang out my truth for the whole world to see. It would say, simply, *Desperate Woman*.

I knew the women were laughing because they could relate. For some it would mean...

- *I am blatantly advertising my need for a husband.*
- *I am at my wit's end.*
- *I am a head case.*

But, as I explained to them, it means something far different to me. You see, for a long time I lived as if I were under water and only occasionally came up for air—then to be pushed down again by my anger, my insecurities, my ache.

When I met Jesus, it was as if I was going for another breath and He scooped me up and carried me as He walked on water. Even now I still feel the storms and the waves. I still wiggle out of His embrace and sink—gasping for air—realizing that when left on my own, I die a slow death. Jesus gives me consistent life. The strength, the new eyes, the wisdom, the love. It's all His life.

I am completely desperate without Him. I sink without Him. Is that weakness? Yes. I am so weak without Him and His presence and guidance. I must get up every day and hold on to hope. Being desperate is something to celebrate because of the position it puts me in with the tender, generous, romantic Lover of my soul. Living a life of passion, romance, and adventure is about panting for

God out of sheer desperation so He can satisfy my deepest longings.

And oh, how deep are my longings! God made me a hungry, thirsty, needy woman. He made all of us that way so that we would seek out His richest fare, as if our lives depended on it—because they do. There is nothing wrong with the intensity of our needs and desires. We just need to remember where the banquet is so we don't end up in the hog pen with nothing but slop and cornhusks.

"It is only the Lord's mercies that have kept us from complete destruction." That's how *The Living Bible* translates Lamentations 3:22. *Complete destruction?* Isn't that a bit too dramatic? I mean, people are basically good, aren't they? Well…actually no. God says no. That's why we need a Savior.

Take a close look at a one-year-old. Not long enough on this earth to develop any real bad habits, right? Wrong, obviously. We are wired, as human beings, to want our way—and to scream and yell if we don't get it. Straight out of the womb we start sobbing, begging to be put back in our warm, cozy place. And that's normal. Unfortunately, we take that same infantile approach into our adult lives and too easily forget Jesus along the way. We try to get back to something familiar and safe, but we go in the wrong direction. As a result, we're...

- never quite at home
- never quite fulfilled
- never quite loved enough

It's easy to end up just "never quite" living our lives. We go on searching and reaching and grabbing and clawing for happiness and satisfaction. We drink and drink and are still parched. We eat and eat as our very souls waste away from starvation. It's as though we keep yelling out for God but remain deaf to His gentle voice: *I am right here.*

I was at a women's event and was passing a line of tables filled with books and Bible studies. One in particular caught my eye. It had a one-word title: *Why?* A tear was dripping from the bottom of the letter *y*. How simple yet powerful the meaning of that cover was. It represented everyone on this earth who has a pulse. It is the cry of our hearts amidst the pain.

I thought about the thousands of times that it was the only word I spoke to God when I couldn't utter anything else. I thought about how many times people I love have spoken that same word. "Why?" enters the heavens and heads straight into His throne room, and I believe those cries hit merciful ears.

Although God holds the future and sees the whole of eternity, He knows that we have limited ability to process His plans and purposes. He knows that we get focused on our pain and not on Him. Our problems cloud His promises. Scripture says that we see with veiled faces. Our vision is blurred. We forget that whatever the need is, He will be the provision. Missionary James Hudson Taylor wrote, "I have found that there are three stages in every great work of God: first it is impossible, then it is difficult, then it is done."

- God said it would rain. Noah believed Him.
  Everyone else laughed. The water came down
  in buckets.

- Joseph was betrayed by his brothers. He spent eleven years as a slave and two years in prison. He went from those confines to Pharaoh's palace and became governor of Egypt.
- Lazarus was Jesus' dear friend. When Jesus heard Lazarus was dead, He waited three days to see him. No one understood. Then Jesus came and called him back to life.
- Jesus hung on a cross. He was mocked and tortured. All seemed hopeless. He rose from the dead three days later.

All of these situations involved waiting. As followers of Jesus, it's no different for us. But something happens to us in the wait, if we let it. The apostle Peter described that something in beautiful terms: "And the God of all grace, who called you to his eternal glory in Christ, after you have suffered a little while, will himself restore you and make you strong, firm and steadfast" (1 Peter 5:10).

The people I know who have waited on God and trusted Him in their pain *are* strong, firm, and steadfast. They are living proof to me of the words of Bishop Handley Moule: "There is no situation so chaotic that God cannot—from that situation—create something that is surpassingly good. He did it at creation. He did it at the cross. He is doing it today."

God knows exactly where we are in our pain. He sees us and reaches out with great compassion. There have been times in my life where I have said, "Don't You see me, Lord? I'm here…"

I have so often heard Him say, *"I know that's where you are, but come with Me."*

I think the Lord would love for us to ask one more question after "Why?" He knows that we will ask that question as long as we struggle here on earth. But I have learned that He longs to hear the next question: "What do I do now, Jesus? Please reveal Yourself to me."

We don't know, but He does. We can't see, and He can. We can trust Him in the midst of things that make no sense. God is big enough to do things that we have labeled impossible. And because God is hope, we must never let go of His hand and all that He represents.

God said that He is the great "I AM." That means He isn't "I was." He isn't "I maybe." We surely can find hope in that. He never has an "off day." He will not change.

God *can't* break his word. And because his word cannot change, the promise is likewise unchangeable.

We who have run for our very lives to God have every reason to grab the promised hope with both hands and never let go. It's an unbreakable spiritual lifeline, reaching past all appearances right to the very presence of God. (Hebrews 6:18-19, MSG)

"I think all Christians would agree with me," C. S. Lewis wrote, "if I said that though Christianity seems at first to be all about morality, all about duties and rules and guilt and virtue, yet it leads you on, out of all that, into something beyond."

I yearn for my life to possess the "something beyond." The something beyond the pain. The something beyond the rain. Fortunately, God answers the cry of my heart and leads me on. Every morning I need to remember to push open the doors of my heart and let God in. When I do that, I remain conscious of Him and the day always takes a different turn. I can process happenings through

His grid and have much less angst. I can keep the hope in my heart alive because I have let hope in.

Sometimes I wish I could be with Him. I mean physically hold Christ's hand. Climb onto His lap and let Him hold me. I marvel at the intimacy that the apostle John had with Jesus. At the Last Supper, Scripture says that John reclined next to Jesus at the table. To be that close! When we know Him, isn't that a great desire of our hearts?

I recorded a song several years ago written by Chris Rice. I sobbed the first time I heard it. I thought that Chris must have peeked into my heart and saw my longing, or surely he had heard my conversations with God.

I heard about the day You went away
You said You had to go prepare a place
And even though I've never seen Your face
I'm missin' You

I lie awake tonight and I watch the sky
And I wish it didn't have to be so high
'Cause I'm belonging on the other side
And I'm missin' You...

I dream about Your promise to return
And I wake up hangin' on Your every word
But for now my feet are planted here on
      earth
So I'm missin' You

And even though they say that I'm a fool
I know You see me waiting here for You
Oh, and prayin' that somehow You'll get
      here soon
'Cause I'm missin' You[1]

And yet even with all the intense longing, I know that He gave His Holy Spirit to us for our greater good. He went away visibly so that we could find Him and have Him invisibly—anytime and anywhere.

When Jesus gave the Great Commission to the eleven disciples after He rose from the dead, He lifted up His hands and blessed them. What comforting words the Lord spoke as He was taken up into heaven: "And surely I am with you always, to the very end of the age" (Matthew 28:20).

Can you imagine what the disciples felt at that moment? What thoughts raced through their minds as they truly understood who He was and what He had done for them.

Louis Evely wrote so magnificently:

> For three years
>> God had lived with them,
>> God had eaten at their table,
>> God had slept in their homes,
>> God had told them about Himself—
>>> And they'd never even thanked Him.
> Now they saw how rude and thoughtless they'd
>> been;
> they saw everything they could've done for
>> Him,
>> everything they could've said,
>> all the happiness they could've given
>>> Him.
> "And they stood there, gazing up into heaven."

Heaven'd begun thirty-three years before,
    and they hadn't noticed.

But angels came to shake them,
    rouse them from their nostalgia
and send them into the world,
      where their Master was waiting
        for them.
It wasn't too late, they realized.
      Now they could do for men
        all they were sorry they hadn't done
          for Christ.
      Together, they'd renew the great Adventure
        that'd never end.
      They were going to live heaven on earth.[2]

When I first read these lines, it seemed a mirror was held up to my soul. I saw clearly what I could learn from the disciples. I don't want life to pass me by, and I realize how many times I missed out on the Lord's will because of my unbelief. I don't want people I love to get short-changed because I got in the way of Jesus. I don't want to be so bound up by the troubles in this world that I leave Him waiting with outstretched hands of hope, yearning to free me and place me in the center of His will.

When the Lord told Moses that He wanted him to lead the Israelites out of Egypt, with all the fear and insecurity and anxiety Moses must have felt at that moment, God said, "I will certainly be with you" (Exodus 3:12, NKJV). That's the same message Jesus gave as He was leaving for heaven. I know that He doesn't mind saying them again for you and me:

"I lost my husband."
"I will certainly be with you."

"I am suffering with depression."
"I will certainly be with you."

"I have cancer."
"I will certainly be with you."

"My child is in trouble."
"I will certainly be with you."

With any burden you lay before God, you can be certain of what He will speak into the depths of your heart. Psalm 23:4 says, "Though I walk through the valley of the shadow of death…" Many times when we have read this verse we ignore the *shadow* and focus on the *death*." David used the word *shadow* because there is no shadow without light. There is always light amidst the pain—because He will never leave us. Even in the darkness there will always be light.

I have been outside in the middle of the night. Pitch black. But the beauty of the brilliant stars in the sky fills my heart with sweet life. I am reminded that life is so much bigger than I. That is the heart attitude I want in the darkness. The darkness will always come. But I have learned so much in the dark. At times God puts us through the discipline of darkness to teach us to heed Him. Songbirds are taught to sing in the dark, and we are put in the shadow of God's hand until we learn to hear Him.

I will give you the treasures of darkness,
    riches stored in secret places,
so that you may know that I am the LORD,

the God of Israel, who summons you by
name. (Isaiah 45:3)

I am a rich woman because I can truly feel forgiveness
and love. I cry with compassion and mercy. I yearn to give
myself away, and hopefully, most of that will be the life
of Christ. I have often become rich after being in the
dark. The loss of my parents, my food addiction, my self-
contempt, my lusts—all of this pain has been used to
deposit God's riches into my bank account, both on earth
and in heaven. Without the darkness, I would not be the
woman I have become.

He invites you to live a life of hope. A life fulfilled.
And when those days come when it takes energy just to
take another breath, hope is just a glance away. It is one
look at Jesus. Hold on to Him. Hold on to hope.

And yes, I am a desperate woman. I pray I will keep
that pin on until He takes it off in heaven.

Way Up High

The danger for most of us lies not in setting our aim too high and falling short, but in setting our aim too low and achieving our mark.

MICHELANGELO

*A*pretty sweet thing happened yesterday as I was trying to find the words to conclude this book. I ran some errands and came home to find a package had been delivered to my front door. It was addressed to *Aunt Kathleen Troccoli.*

I smiled as I picked it up and carried it in. It was from my niece, Maria, a glorious twenty-two-year-old who absolutely delights my soul. One of the greatest compliments I have ever received was when one of our friends asked her, "So, tell me, what do you love about your aunt?"

I almost sobbed as Maria replied, "Well, she has taught me that I can live a romantic life."

My relationship with my nieces has been a priority ever since they were little girls. Back then I lived in Nashville, and my mother was still alive. They saw her every day. She adored them. When she died, they were about six and seven, and I felt like God was urging me to really "lean in" because my sister and their father are divorced. The girls have a pretty good relationship with their dad now, but they had two big losses at one time—a divorce and the loss of their grandmother, who was truly their best friend. My sister became a working single mom, and she did her best to provide for them and help them know Jesus.

I made sure I was there for the holidays, especially on Christmas Eve. They always knew that I would wake up with them on Christmas morning and that there would be something under the Christmas tree. I pursued their hearts and interests and allowed them to talk to me about anything. I was there for them when they called me. I would listen to the tears and frustration. I would talk to them about the importance of kindness. I would talk to them about being substantial young women and how they could make a difference in the world—and that their lives could go beyond ordinary to extraordinary. They are beautiful and delightful. They are growing, and I delight in all I see the Lord doing with each of them.

So, since it was close to my birthday, I knew this was some sort of gift. I opened it up to find the movie *Robin Hood: Prince of Thieves* starring Kevin Costner. On top of the package was a card with a picture of Judy Garland as Dorothy in *The Wizard of Oz*. Here's what the card said:

Dear Aunt Kathleen,

I love you,

I love you!

And I am so incredibly proud of you!

Mommy, Gina, and I are giving you a present from all of us—but this is just a little something from me! You probably haven't seen it in a while, but I just recently saw it for the first time in a while. And Aunt Kathleen, this is the type of man we want! [Mind you I am forty-seven and she is twenty-two. How precious is that?]

I bought two—one for me and one for you! Watch it and experience the magic of fantasy that maybe one day will be reality. Get chills, feel the butterflies, and dream away!

All my love.

Happy Birthday to an incredibly accomplished woman!

His,

Ri

I marvel. It is amazing what God can do in a woman's heart. Despite what I saw this little girl go through, she has grown up to be a marvelous young woman. We certainly live in a paradox of existence between earth and heaven. But if you lean toward heaven, it leans back. The love, the beauty, the hope. It is all there.

No one will be exempt from sorrow. No one will be able to dodge the pain that pours onto the earth and into the hearts of all of us. It is a fact. We are not in the garden. But there is great truth to the phrase, "Life is what you make it." It comes down to whether we are inviting and embracing the input and influence of God in the midst of our journey. Darkness is never completely dark when the light of God breaks through. And we can always have the hope of a new day and a new place to arrive.

> For lo, the winter is past,
>> The rain is over and gone.
>> The flowers appear on the earth;
>> The time of singing has come.
>> (Song of Solomon 2:11-12, NKJV)

Well, as you can tell by now, my little telephone conversation with Paris caused me to do some thinking and lots of writing. It is my heart's desire to continue to gain all the eternal riches that I can this side of heaven. It is like being at an Italian wedding. The music will play and someone will start a conga line. Before you know it, half of the people in the room join in. It infects the crowd with fun and laughter. That is the kind of passionate, romantic, adventurous life God wants us to lead. I don't want to sit the dance out. I don't want to watch from my chair. I am determined to get up and live to the fullest and look behind me and see the line getting longer and longer with all those who take hold of the abundant life God so generously offers to us.

> Somewhere over the rainbow
> Way up high
> There's a land that I heard of
> Once in a lullaby[1]

Where is "way up high"? It's like we are always getting ready to live and making plans to live—hoping to live but never really living. It's like we keep dreaming about that "somewhere over the rainbow," and if we just looked out our window, we would see one hanging over our own backyard. This land doesn't have to be one you've "heard of." You can move into it and live in it as you follow God's lead. Don't settle and watch other people live your dreams. He yearns for you to live into them.

A rich, passionate, romantic, adventurous God invites you to engage, to enjoy, to participate with zest and abandon in the life He has given you. Take the hand of the Lover of your soul to somewhere over the rainbow. Live like you mean it!

Notes

An Invitation

1. "Over the Rainbow," by Harold Arlen and E. Y. Harburg, © 1938 (renewed 1966) Metro-Goldwyn-Mayer, © 1939 (renewed 1967) EMI Feist Catalog Inc. All rights reserved. Used by permission.
2. Keith Green, "Asleep in the Light," BMG Songs Inc., 1981.

Chapter 3

1. Kathy Troccoli, "A Different Road," Sony/ATV Songs, 1998. All rights reserved. Used by permission.
2. Attributed to Martha Snell Nicholson. For one Internet reference see www.desiringgod.org/library/sermons/01/051301.html.

Chapter 4

1. Ken Gire, *Windows of the Soul* (Grand Rapids: Zondervan, 1996).

2. Louis Evely, *That Man Is You*, trans. Edmond Bonin (New York: Newman, 1968), 16-17.

3. "There's Something About That Name." Words by William J. and Gloria Gaither. Music by William J. Gaither. Copyright © 1970 William J. Gaither Inc. All rights controlled by Gaither Copyright Management. Used by permission.

Chapter 7

1. Chris Rice, "Missing You," © 1995 BMG Songs (ASCAP). All rights administered BMG Songs (ASCAP). Used by permission.

2. Louis Evely, *That Man Is You*, trans. Edmond Bonin (New York: Newman, 1968), 289-90.

Another Invitation

1. "Over the Rainbow," by Harold Arlen and E. Y. Harburg, © 1938 (renewed 1966) Metro-Goldwyn-Mayer, © 1939 (renewed 1967) EMI Feist Catalog Inc. All rights reserved. Used by permission.

About the Author

Contemporary pop was taking center stage for the first time in Christian music in 1982, and after shopping for a record deal, the founders of Reunion Records decided to start their own label to launch the music career of an Italian girl from New York, **KATHY TROCCOLI.**

Kathy has come a long way since her musical debut, but her passion for sharing the gospel and her life through music has not waned. She recently completed her sixteenth album release, *Comfort,* which features songs specifically designed to bring comfort and peace in difficult times. Kathy's own intimate relationship with God is evident through the production style, which features only piano, guitar, and her trademark voice.

Not only has Kathy found herself continuing her successful music career, but she has grown as a speaker as well. Her effective communication style, funny stories, and passionate way of living have made her a favorite among women around the world. She appears before packed houses with Women of Faith, Heritage Keepers,

Time Out for Women and other key women's conferences. Her concerts and speaking engagements, which put her in front of over two hundred thousand people a year, include her own popular conference with Dee Brestin: *Falling in Love with Jesus*.

The diverse talents and circumstances in Kathy's life have also made it possible for her to motivate others through the written word. She has allowed the successes and trials she has encountered to mold her over the years, equipping her for a multifaceted career. *A Love that Won't Walk Away* and *Falling in Love with Jesus* are among her published works. *Live Like You Mean It* is her eighth book.

"The good and the bad have been helpful in deepening my relationship with God," says Kathy. "I feel like everything that's happened in my life has brought me to this point for a purpose, and I long to share that hope with others."